TO LIVE
AS JESUS DID

A Handbook for Christian Living

Rev. Bernard C. Hayes, C.R.

LIVING FLAME PRESS
LOCUST VALLEY, N.Y. 11560

Cover Design: Robert Manning

Nihil Obstat: Rev. John Barker, J.C.L., S.T.L., *Censor Librorum,* January 6, 1981.

Imprimatur: Thomas J. McDonough, D.D., J.C.D., Archbishop of Louisville, January 6, 1981.

Published by: Living Flame Press / Locust Valley / New York 11560

ISBN: 0-914544-35-7

Printed in the United States of America

Dedication

I gratefully dedicate this book to the Staff of St. Thomas Center, to my fellow religious in the Congregation of the Resurrection and to all those who by their sharing in so many ways have taught me something of what it means to live as Jesus did.

Acknowledgements

A book is always the product of many hands. Every writer owes a huge debt of gratitude to those without whose help he would be unable to share his thoughts. I acknowledge my debt to the many friends who have helped me by loving me over the years; Sister Mary Matthias Ward, O.S.U., and Reverend William C. Hartlage of the Staff at St. Thomas Center, Louisville, Kentucky, for their patient endurance and helpful suggestions; to Mrs. Pat Lambert and Mrs. Pat Mattingly for their diligent work in typing the manuscript; to Sister Marilyn Mueller, O.S.U., for her technical assistance and to all those from whom I have drawn inspiration and strength.

Biblical quotations have been taken from *The New English Bible* and the *Good News Bible*.

Table of Contents

Table of Contents

Introduction

A friend of mine remarked recently that she once asked some of her companions why they never spoke about God. The answer: "Because talk about God reminds us of death." With some astonishment, my friend replied, "But God is *life!* Jesus can teach us how to *live!*" That is what the following pages are all about. They are an invitation to see the essentials of life as Jesus saw them, to accept and live life as he did. That is the theme of this book.

The basis of Jesus' life was always humble and loving submission to the will of his Father as the Father revealed it to him. The basis of our lives must be the same. We must pray to know the will of our Father for us; be open to receiving it; answer its call to rebirth; see it at work in our failures and successes, our need for comforting and healing, for forgiving and being forgiven. For us, as for Jesus, our Father's will must be that "food" which others may perhaps not know.

Except for Jesus, no other person so fully responded to God's call and His will as our Blessed Mother did. That is why this book ends with a chapter on Mary. She is our finest statement — and our surest hope.

Life is at the same time man's greatest gift and his greatest challenge. Although it is extremely difficult to live well and sometimes a struggle just to exist, as followers of Jesus Christ, we are called upon not only to live life but to live it well — to make the life which Jesus lived our blueprint. In our approach to the major events of our existence we must always "put on the mind of the Lord Jesus." In that lies our inspiration, our example and hope.

Like ourselves, Jesus was called to cope with his experiences. St. Paul writes that Jesus "was a man, like us in all things but sin." No one knew life as Jesus knew it. No one ever marched so surely through life to the "beat of a different drummer."

The beat which guided Jesus, and must guide us too, is the constant pulse of love: "The Father loves you." Jesus spent his days continually in the light of his Father's love for him and for us all and committed himself to the fullest possible return of that love. If we would be Jesus' followers, that light must guide our path as well; that commitment must become our own. *To Live As Jesus Did* is an attempt to focus on our daily routine and to see through the eyes of Jesus the basic purpose and meaning of life itself and of some major events common to all human experience.

It is impossible to capture every facet of our existence in one book. There is no single detailed and complete plan for living; our lives are too

8

varied for that. But it is possible to offer some insights, drawn from experience, on the Christian approach to those events common to all and with which we are all required to cope. What is the significance for the Christian of birth and death; of success and failure; of sin and forgiveness? It is imperative that our attitude towards these life-elements be a reflection of Jesus' attitude. By focusing-in however briefly on these events, we hopefully will, with Jesus, come to see them in the fullness of their meaning and purpose. We can then learn to integrate them and use them as the instruments of growth they are meant to be.

The sole purpose of this book, then, is to lead the reader to a clearer vision of the value and purpose of these common events. Each chapter is an entity in itself. The link uniting all of the chapters is life as seen through Jesus' eyes, and each one deals with an experience. Each is an attempt at a better understanding, a spring-board from which, by his own prayer and reflection, the reader may find those answers which best suit his being and in those answers find God more fully.

A storyteller has one of his characters say to his beloved: "I never knew what life meant until I saw it in your eyes." If the reader is led to perceive the true meaning of life by seeing it in and with the eyes of Jesus, this simple book will have fulfilled its purpose.

1

Our Common Journey

This is really a "how to" book.

Over the years I have had to face for myself and with others many of the "how to" questions of life and living. Given their universal nature, I am sure a number of these same questions are part of your experience. In general they go like this: How do I handle failure? What is the purpose and sense of life anyway? What is joy and how is it found? What does it mean to be "reborn"? Does suffering have any real value? How can I be truly successful without being destroyed by my success? Is forgiveness important? Is it even really possible? Why do we die?

Having had to struggle in learning to cope with these and similar questions, I eventually saw that I was not unique in that endeavor and that others might profit from my study, my struggles and my conclusions. I felt I had to share the "good news" which I had discovered. Hence this book.

Over the years, I have talked at length with psychologists, participated in innumerable courses, workshops and programs and read all sorts of "how

to" books: *How to Deal With Tension and Stress;
How to Weather the Various Stages of Psychological
Growth; How to Achieve Happiness Through This
or That; How to Find Your Erroneous Zones,* etc.
Some of these helped but did not really end my
search. Others were no help at all.

It dawned on me one day that I was, at least in
name, a Christian. Would that fact help in my
search for peace and meaning? Was there something in Christianity which would bring my being
and its complexities into focus and free me to
enter into that fullness of life I sought? I decided
to see.

One day while reading the Scriptures, my attention was aroused by this passage from the
First Letter of John: "Here is the test by which
we can make sure that we are in him: whoever
claims to be dwelling in him, binds himself to live
as Jesus did" (1 John 2:6).

Was that the answer I sought? Was I really
dwelling in him as I claimed to be? Did I allow
Jesus to permeate my spirit or was I merely com-
partmentalizing my life — planning this part for
work, that for recreation, another for my career
and finally one more separate part for the Lord,
for my "spiritual" life?

The longer I thought, the more convinced I became of the latter. In a great many areas of my
life I simply did not commit myself to live as Jesus
did. I had set up a division within myself (a small
part Christian, the largest part not) which could
only lead to inner warfare. In that state, true

11

peace of mind was impossible.

"But," I asked myself, "what does it mean to live as Jesus lived?" Withdrawing from the inevitable soul-searching posed by this question, I asked the more basic one: "What does it mean to live? What are those components, integral to every life, by which our being can commonly be described and circumscribed?" Certainly among these we must list birth, joy, sorrow, success, failure, sin, forgiveness and a sense of purpose, a mission. Did Christianity deal with these? Did Jesus face these same questions, sufferings and doubts; did he show me the "how to" I was seeking? I resolved to read the scriptures carefully in an attempt to see just how Jesus lived.

To truly see, I laid aside temporarily the divinity of our Lord in order to perceive him more objectively and sharply as one like myself. The longer I delved into the person Jesus and dwelt on his life and teaching, the more clearly I was able to identify with him, to appreciate his humanity as well as his divinity. I began to understand him, to relate to him, to draw close to him. With this increased closeness came increased healing and peace, new insight, deeper perceptivity and a more integrated existence. Life became worth living. Peace, joy, contentment and happiness not only ceased to remain mere words but grew increasingly as realities. So much of my darkness began to give way to light that I could at last realize the ineffable happiness I now experience: my heart is incapable of containing all the joy I feel and my cup runneth over.

The following pages are an attempt to trace the difficulties and joys encountered up to this point in my journey through the efforts I made to follow Jesus by modelling my life on his.

Given the inherent obstinacy of my own will, the Lord has not always been able to lead me gently. Sometimes he has had to push and pull me into that growth which I so easily avoided. My growth is not complete nor has the Lord ceased to push and pull. If at times this guidance remains intensely painful, it never fails to bring greater insight, clearer vision and an abundance of joy.

Our journeys, yours and mine, in life and in faith are essentially the same. Perhaps in sharing with you some of my own encounters, my efforts, successes and failures, and the insight which came to me through prayer, I can be of help as you continue your own struggle to live as Jesus did, to experience the wonder and fullness of life.

2

"Come Follow Me . . ."

When the Father sent Jesus to this world as a "man, like us in all things but sin," he did not change the rules to make living easier for his Son. Jesus freely chose to live his life, bound by the same rules or conditions that the Father imposed on all his creatures. In his humanity, Jesus truly joined us on this battlefield we call life.

When Jesus invites us to follow him he is calling us to much more than a superficial change in our way of living. Jesus knows what life is about and what living entails. He does not call us to discipleship in the way one might invite a friend to join a club. The two disciples who asked Jesus to show them where he lived quite probably got more than they were asking for. Jesus' reply to them, "come and see," invited them to see a great deal more than simply his physical dwelling, for Jesus would spend the next three momentous years trying to show them and us, that "where" he truly "lived" was in the love and the will of his Father whose image among men he was sent to manifest.

If we accept our invitation to follow Jesus, the

terms are his, not ours. To be a Christian does **not** mean to live a "new" or "different" life but rather to live *this* life *anew;* that is, with fresh and vitalizing insights into its purpose, meaning and basis. If one is to live Christianity, he must continually grow toward that still-point of being where the question: "Why do I exist?" coalesces with that of: "What does the Father will for me?" and the two become one. This process must begin in God and, since God is love, it must spring from love. A Christian is born when one understands that the secret of being is love, that there can be no distinction between loving and living for anyone who would experience that fullness of life which the Father is so anxious to share. The key to Jesus' wholehearted embracing of humanity, to the ease with which he submits in all things to his Father's will for him, is the knowledge that his whole life is an expression of love: his love for the Father and the Father's love for him. For Jesus, existence has no other basis, no other purpose, no fuller meaning. No other is needed.

Throughout his whole life, the Father is the person who is paramount to Jesus. What did his Father want? When he discovered that the Father willed for him to show men the fullness of his (the Father's) redeeming love, Jesus never hesitated, never stopped to count the cost, never demanded any assurances that his life and love would not be given in vain. For Jesus, union with the Father was enough and his knowledge that the Father truly loved him was more than sufficient return for the toil, heartbreaks, and suffering that the living out of his Father's love required of him. In his love he trusted and with that trust he was able to walk to Calvary and beyond.

Anyone who would truly accept Jesus' invitation to discipleship must, before all else, be prepared, as Jesus was, to become fully a lover. To stop short of loving freely, totally and spontaneously is to remain on the fringe of the crowd at best. Only when we allow our love of the Father to become increasingly real and intense can we claim to have begun our life's journey in imitation of the Lord.

Only one who perceives that he is loved can truly fall in love. The Good News cries out: "Hear, O man, your God loves you." And to this tremendous news, Jesus invites us to respond: "I love you, Father!"

The implications of this good news and its inherent call are mind-boggling. It all seems simply too good to be true! The Father loves me! The Father calls me to love him! What could be simpler? Yet we are so often left wondering what it all means. It is indeed a great and mysterious revelation. Its realization, its understanding must be found by prayer and reflection.

This understanding is not always easily acquired. Because of events and people in my past, I lived a long time before really believing that God loved me for myself, for the "me" who is truly there and not the person I felt compelled to pretend existed. For years my self-acceptance was tied to success, position, authority. I felt my need for approval would be satisfied if I could be accepted not for "who" I was but for "what" I was. I was so convinced that I was right that I rejected many hands held out to me in love. Since I did not see myself as loveable, I saw no real need for love. In fact love was a threat. Any approach made out of love was viewed with suspicion. I was firmly convinced that love was needless humbug and that people who spoke to me endearingly were simply trying to manipulate me. Their well-meant advances were sternly rejected. I remember distinctly the first time anyone felt free enough to say to me: "I love you." My reaction was one of shocked embarrassment and instant rejection. I simply did not know how to handle that basic statement. My immediate thought was: "I wonder what that person wants."

Only the knowledge that we are loveable, that we can truly love and be loved, can enable us to be honestly self-accepting, open, truthful with ourselves and others. The truth that makes us free is the knowledge that we are loved, always loved, no matter what. This is God's great gift to us and it comes, as so many of his gifts, through and from the hands and hearts of others. When we truly realize and accept the reality of another's love for us, we can begin to accept God's love. In the genuine love of another we find our true self-esteem. With the knowledge that I am loveable, I can open my eyes and see the love in my life, and the need others have for my love; then I can believe in God's love for me. I can begin to trust. A wall-hanging at my place of work reads: "If I bare myself to you, do not laugh at my nakedness." That is the heart and the fruit of my realized "lovedness." It is a freeing from that narrow and constricted closing-in on self which is the inevitable result of feeling unloveable and of not daring to see ones' self as sprung from and destined for love alone.

In this process, true friendship is indispensable. I can never be truly convinced of my loveableness until I have found a special someone to love me and whom I can truly love. God loves me in the concrete as well as in the abstract. Until I have found someone against whom I can kick and scream and rail, on whose shoulder I can cry and in whose arms I can be comforted — I cannot actually *know* God's love for me. The existence of that love may indeed be a truth for me but it will be a truth which exists only in the remote depths of my intellect. It will never really touch my life. It will neither sustain nor comfort me. I will truly know God's love for me when he allows it to become incarnated in another on whose constant and unfailing love I can rely in total assurance of his or her fidelity no matter what. "A friend," says St. Augustine, "is one who knows all about you and loves you just the same." A "friend" can be anyone: mother, father, husband, wife or lover, but without a friend I can never really believe in the Father's love for me. Through my friend's love, I not only come to know the Father's love for me, but see, taste and experience it, for through God's love I am reborn.

My life has a purpose, meaning and importance solidly rooted in the Father's love for me. It is so hard to resist being entrapped by non-Christian standards often applied to judge importance: money, power, fame, position, yet I must not allow these secular standards to rob me of my purpose, my dignity, my beauty, my meaning. All these rest in the Father's love for me! "And the secret is that Christ rests in you, your pledge of glory" (Colossians 1:27). This is the basis of my response to the invitation to follow Jesus. My call is above all a deep inner prompting to understand that I am loved and needed.

We are all created out of love. None of us is an "accident." Regardless of the motivation of our parents, we are, each of us, born of the Father's love. It is this love which is to be the basis of our existence and all our activity. "We love," says St. John, "because God first loved us" (1 John 4:19). It is in the total realization of this truth that a human love finds its fulfillment. The first of the Great Commandments calls on us to realize God's love and to return it wholeheartedly. It is the Second of the Great Commandments which calls us to love our neighbor and is radically rooted in the First, so much so indeed that this Second is not really possible unless the First is lived and has primacy. If my love of neighbor is to be genuinely of God, the Second of the Commandments can never supplant the First or supersede it.

The first step then in our journey with Jesus is to root our lives deeply in the love which the Father has for us individually, that love which alone can give genuine meaning and purpose to our lives. This is where Jesus started.

At some point in his history, Jesus came to know the Father's overwhelming love for him. Everything else then became possible. No obstacle was too big; no suffering too great. His earthly existence, determined from all time, had become a reality. Now all else would be guided by the Father's loving hand. Having uttered his irrevocable "yes" from all eternity in the bosom of the Father, Jesus concretizes it, "incarnates" it, in his human existence. He becomes the embodiment of the Father's love, visible for all to see. At some stage of his earthly life, he apprehends the meaning and purpose of his existence. His journey begins in earnest.

Our journey in faith must begin with the same starting point: knowing Jesus and, through him, knowing the Father's love from which we spring. To know with St. Paul the depth and intensity of God's love for us, to trust him and take him at his word — this is the true beginning of our faith-journey, the start of our pilgrimage through this life back to the Father from whom we came. This is the "pearl of great price" before which all else pales in significance. This is the "leaven which 'enleavens' all the rest," our key to peace and joy and love, the summation of all Jesus said, did and stood for. It is to this commitment that Jesus calls us: to know our lives as meaningful because we have been born of love and to show this truth to others so that, with them and through Christ, the Father may be glorified in us. This is the heart of Jesus' call to follow him: that we surrender to love. Jesus challenges us as no one has ever done to become lovers, to fall truly in love with every person who allows us to receive and manifest his life-giving love.

Our Lord's call, his challenge, is a "dangerous" one. Its implications for man are enormous as we shall see. Our decision to answer that call must be free. Love can never be forced. If we accept it we must be prepared to start at the beginning, at birth, where all life begins. We must be "reborn."

"The word of the Lord came to me: Before I formed you in the womb I knew you for my own" (Jeremiah 1:4-5).

3

Birth and Rebirth

All life begins with birth. Our life with Jesus is no exception. If we want to live anew we must be born anew to understand the impact of this rebirth on our lives. Jesus showed great wisdom when he insisted that our rebirth is the indispensable prelude for entry into the "kingdom."

It is a fact of life that one is never simply "born." Each of us is being constantly "reborn": biologically, psychologically and spiritually. Psychologically and spiritually this "rebirth" centers on the questions: "Who am I?" and "Why do I exist?" or "Why was I born?" Our honest willingness to answer these questions will determine the direction our lives will take. Jesus grows "in wisdom and age and grace" as he develops an understanding of who he is and the "why" of his human existence.

Great psychologist that he is, Jesus sees this "rebirth" as indispensable for true entry into discipleship with him. No one can be fully Jesus' disciple unless he is willing to see his existence and his purpose through Jesus' eyes, for he must endeavor to live his life in accord with the truths revealed to him through the insights of faith. I cannot be a true disciple unless I am willing to be "reborn" and to realize all that growing in my life with Jesus entails.

Nowhere does Jesus express this statement more clearly than in the following familiar passage from the Gospel of John: "In reply Jesus said, 'In truth, in very truth I tell you, unless a man has been born over again, he cannot see the Kingdom of God!' " (John 3:3). Modern man often misses the importance and the meaning of this quotation.

For modern man, the question: "Why do I exist?" is so often made to read: "What am I to *do?*" Doing has become all-important. It overshadows being. All too frequently we are judged and our worth is calculated by what we do, by our fame, our wealth, etc. This is a legacy of the utilitarianism which has been inculcated into our society. It is not of God. God never needs us to do, except in a very general sense. Much more importantly, God needs us to *be.*

For many of us, the learning of that simple truth can take a long time and bring untold agony. Throughout much of my life, my vehicle for gaining acceptance by others was accomplishment. I believed that the more I drove myself to perform well, the more others would praise me, depend on me, see me as worthwhile and valuable, and the more I would be accepted by them. In my blindness, fear, and ignorance I drove myself and others relentlessly. I *had* to work, I had to succeed or no one would "love" me. So life became a play. I was the director. All else and all others were props. Ultimately, of course, I broke under the strain of it all. My whole world collapsed. Then a strange and wonderful thing happened. As I sat in the midst of the wreckage, I found love. For the first time I discovered that others could and did love me, not for what I could do, for I was literally unable to do anything, but for who I was and who I could be. Gradually I began to see that my greatest work was to become the best I could be and my greatest contribution to others was my gift of self.

I began to see that unless my "doing" sprang from, reflected and contributed to my "being," it mattered little. People were no longer objects used to achieve my goals. I learned to stop playing the role of a "performer" and began to be a "liver." I had the freedom to become a "lover." I no longer cursed the day I was born. I perceived my pet prop: "After all, I didn't ask to be born," for the cop-out it really was. I took the first halting steps toward living instead of pretending to live; I stopped "rejecting" my life while continuing to "live"; I ceased acting and became real. To reach this point, I had to first see life for what it really is: a *gift*. None of us chose to be born. Our physical birth was the end-product of a whole series of events about which we had no knowledge and over which we had no control. We did not "will" ourselves into existence. In every case, life was the first gift we received.

Somewhere along the line, however, we had to "will" to accept that gift, to make it our own. We had to decide to continue in existence. At first, this "willing" was simply our innate response to the strong instinct for survival which is universal. As we grew older, however, we became increasingly less dominated by the instinctive will to live and more aware of our freedom to choose between preservation or destruction of our life. Concurrently we developed an increased awareness that suffering — even intense suffering — is a large and vital part of our existence. At some point on that continuum we were led to accept or reject life. It was at this point that life became, or failed to become, truly a "gift." A gift is only a gift when it is accepted and treasured. Life is no exception. The decision to embrace life became our "moment of rebirth" in the natural order, our "turning point."

There is, however, a major condition inherent in our decision to live. If we choose to embrace life we must be willing to accept it in its fullness, unconditionally. This is so because we basically have little control over our lives. It is true that we freely make many important decisions, many choices which greatly affect the direction of our life and its sense of purpose. "What kind of person will I be?" "What will I do with my life?" These are inescapable, important and necessary questions. But even here in the complicated area of life-choices our decisions may be, and often are, influenced by extrinsic need or external circumstances. It is not always possible to enjoy freedom of choice. At one stage of my life I "vowed" that nothing and no one would induce me to be a priest. Obviously I was wrong.

It is this insight into lack of control over life that prompted St. Augustine's famous remark: "The fact that our future is hidden from us is a mark of God's mercy." We could hardly face life were it not so. It is, however, precisely because our future remains hidden, that we are forced to unconditionally embrace life, once we decide to embrace it at all. Not knowing with any degree of certainty or detail what our future holds, we are totally unable to direct it, to "control" it. So, having decided that life is indeed worth living, we choose by that very decision to accept life as it comes and to live it day by day. Having decided to continue living, we thereby chose to live all of life, the bitter as well as the sweet. If this were not so, our choice to live would be self-delusion rather than reality. We must always embark on life blindly and with trust.

All we have said so far finds its true parallel in the faith-life of every Christian who models his life on the life of Jesus himself.

Conscious that life is a gift of the Father, given for a purpose, Jesus openly proclaimed his acceptance of the life and mission to which the Father called him. The vehicle he chose for this was his public baptism by John in the Jordan. A few words about this event are in order.

John was not baptizing converts, people who

wished to join the Jewish faith. The people he baptized were already Jews, but Jews who were conscious of their need for conversion and repentance, who were moved by sorrow for past sins and who wanted to symbolize their sorrow and their desire to live renewed lives. For these people, John's baptism was a "second call," a moment of spiritual rebirth. It was not quite the same for Jesus. Jesus had no need for conversion, repentance, or rebirth. Rather, Jesus' baptism by John was a public statement of his mission, of his acceptance of the life the Father had fashioned for him. The importance of Jesus' baptism lies in what it signifies. By his baptism, Jesus openly accepts the commission given him by the Father and publicly, "officially," begins the work he has been assigned to do. His mission is our salvation. His commission is to identify himself so completely with us, to become so totally one with us, that through him "man may become reconciled with God and God with man." Sinless himself and therefore without need for repentance or conversion, Jesus identifies himself entirely with man's sinfulness, highlighting in a magnificent and striking way the sovereignty and love of the Father. In return, the Father glorifies Jesus and in him, all of us! "After baptism Jesus came up out of the water at once, and that moment heaven opened; he saw the Spirit of God descending like a dove to alight upon him; and a voice from heaven was heard saying, 'This is my Son, my Beloved, on whom my favor rests' " (Matthew 3:16-17).

The moment of his baptism and its meaning remain with Jesus throughout his life. He will hark back many times to this event and its full significance. Having accepted the purpose of his life, Jesus can go forward to its fulfillment. His life will be ruled by his perception: "I am come not to do my own will but the will of the One who sent me."

Everything we have said of Jesus' baptism is true of our baptism as well; it is our public acceptance of our life in faith, of our faith-purpose.

Baptism is not simply the "cancelling" of sin. More importantly it is a statement of intent, the concretizing of a basic life-choice. It is a public statement of faith, of a faith which acknowledges the interpersonal relationship of God and man and the meaning and purposefulness of man's existence.

While most of us were too young to make this choice, to understand and declare this meaning at the moment of our sacramental baptism, somewhere along the road of our spiritual journey we must do so. At some moment in our history, we must each decide whether our unwilled sacramental baptism will mean anything or not. Just as at some point in time we had to decide to accept or reject physical life, so at a given moment we will be called to do the same with our God-given life in Jesus. The choice will be ours.

Our "yes" to our life in Jesus must be total. If it is to be sincere, it must be complete, irrevocable, unconditional. Without this "yes" in all its fullness, there can be no true rebirth. There can be no living in Jesus either. "I would that you were either hot or cold, but since you are lukewarm, neither hot nor cold, I will spit you out of my mouth" (Revelation 3:17).

The fullness and effectiveness of my life in the Lord will depend on how strong and deliberate my choice to live in him has been. I can drift through life or I can live life. The difference between these choices is great and crucial.

Having made a faith-choice, having decided to be reborn with a faith-based understanding of the value, purpose and plan of life, there remains for us as it did for Jesus, the day by day living out of the inner meaning of our baptism, the daily "incarnation" of its total reality and significance.

My "birth" through baptism into the spiritual life may have been as unwilled by me as my birth into natural life. If, however, I am to live a purposeful and fruitful existence, then the embracing of my "new" life, my acceptance of this gift of faith, must be eagerly willed. God is love and love does not force. It simply invites; it offers. We are free to accept or refuse the gift of life love offers. That choice is always ours. If we accept, we enter into a particular relationship with God. He calls us in love to be his extended family, the modern-day incarnation of the One Son in whom his love so totally reposed.

> "Praise be to the God and Father of our Lord Jesus Christ, who in his great mercy gave us a new birth into a living hope by the resurrection of Jesus Christ from the

dead! The inheritance to which we are
born is one that nothing can destroy or
spoil or wither. It is kept for you in heaven
and you, because of your faith in God, are
under the protection of his power until salvation comes; the salvation which is even
now in readiness and will be revealed at the
end of time" (1 Peter 1:3-5).

4

"The Father and I Are One . . ."

So far our concern has been to stress the following personal realization. If my life is to be modeled on Jesus' life, I must be assured that the Father loves me for myself and that true happiness will come through accepting life as it unfolds, because that is the will of my loving Father.

Whenever we enter into love, however, a relationship is automatically set up. This association may be one of marriage, of family ties, of friendship, etc. Whatever its form, since love always seeks union, some sort of alliance will be established between the lover and the person loved.

If we are truly desirous of living as Jesus lived, there must be some clear-cut and easily definable relationship between us and the Father, just as there was between Jesus and the Father. In all accuracy and fullness of meaning, Jesus could and did say that he and the Father are one, not only because of the perfect union of their wills but also for the reason that in a real sense Jesus is the "natural" son of the Father.

Our situation is different. While it may be true to say that in a very broad sense we too are the "natural" children of God, because of our sinful state, it is more accurate to see ourselves as his by election, or adoption.

What exactly does being "adopted" by God mean in our daily living?

We know that in human society, children are adopted according to a clearly defined process. When the prospective adopting parents have met all the necessary requirements, the child they seek to adopt becomes legitimately theirs.

After our sacramental baptism we become "lawfully" the "adopted" children of our heavenly Father. On our behalf, our parents (or godparents) entered into a "legal contract" with God, whereby without relinquishing their place in our life, they brought us into a formal relationship with the Father. We each became in a real and official sense "a child of God."

In and of itself, however, that probably meant very little if anything at all. Those of us who were baptized as infants were hardly in a position to appreciate and make our own what happened at our baptism. We were not even aware of what was going on. My baptism did not "make" me a child of God except in the very formal sense of "make" which we have just discussed. What it did was give me the power truly to become a child of God, should that be my desire later on in life. This is true of any situation involving adoption. If the adoption is really to become a fact and not remain

32

just a legal fiction, love must somewhere enter the picture. And no one can "make" me love. Love is always the result of free choice. If my adoption by God is really to mean anything to me, then it will never be enough that at my baptism God "adopted" me. Somewhere along the line I must freely and willingly "adopt" God. I must choose independently to enter into some kind of personal association with God. If this does not happen, my alliance with the Father will remain simply "legal." Such an impersonal relationship will obviously have little if any influence on the way I live. It can certainly never be the basis of a life patterned on the life of our Lord.

The type of union we will establish with the Father will depend on the image we have of him. Who is God to me? If he is only someone to be feared, then the relationship I establish with him will be one of fear. If God is simply the provider of "goodies," a sort of divine Santa Claus, then my devotion to him will reflect that. How I perceive God is crucial to my association with him. Only when I see God for what he really is, true and total life-giving LOVE, will I be able to enter fully into a genuine union with him. God will then become for me my own Father and I will become his true child. The "adopted" will disappear from my vocabulary.

A couple who are very close to me adopted two children to whom they gave equal love. Both children are now grown. One of them is very close to her parents. In talking to her it soon becomes very

33

clear that regardless of what her parents are to her legally, they are not "adopted" parents in her eyes. This couple does not even know the whereabouts of their other adopted child. As long as he feared their authority, as long as he "needed" them, he stayed with them. He never returned their love, never really became their son. As soon as he was able, he left. The only contact he had with them came when he needed money or some other assistance. Very reluctantly they once refused him. He does not call or write anymore.

What happened of course is that the girl entered into a love relationship with her adopted parents and the boy did not. Because of the girl's love for them, her parents became "real" to her. The boy never returned the love he was given, never "adopted" the couple who cared enough to adopt him. They did not become real to him. His relationship with them always remained superficial, existing solely on the level of fear, need or necessity. For his part, it was easily terminated.

In similar situations it is not the fact of adoption which makes the difference. It is the presence or absence of felt love on the part of both child and parent. Many "natural" parents could tell the same story.

To be one with the Father therefore means a great deal more than simply entering into the formal relationship with him of having at some time been baptized. To be truly one with God, to share meaningfully in the adoptive act, requires that we see God as much more than our "legal" guardian and protector.

It was precisely this attitude of a legalized relationship with God into which many Jews of Jesus' time had fallen. Their relationship with the Father had become a matter of scrupulous attention to his law as it had been handed down to them. Fidelity to God's law therefore constituted the fullness of religion; membership in God's family was simply a matter of the rite of circumcision. It was this attitude that caused Jesus to lose patience with them so often because for him, meaningful union with the Father could never spring from mere observance of the requirements of the law, no matter how faithful or well-intentioned. He believed that the only valid basis for man's relationship with the Father was knowledge and love. When these are the foundation, law will take care of itself. "He who has God for his Father listens to the words of God. You are not God's children; that is why you do not listen" (John 8:47). These words of our Lord assume even greater significance when one remembers that they were addressed to Jews who boasted of not needing Jesus because they were by law the "children of Abraham" and thereby legal children of God.

Jesus goes to great lengths to point out that it is knowledge of the Father and love for him which form the true basis of fruitful adoption, of our Father-child relationship with God. This is the "revolutionary" message of Jesus which so many would not, and will not, hear. It is really a very simple message: the Father knows and loves you and wants to be known and loved by you. He wants you to be his son, his daughter; in fact, not just in name.

To enter from this conviction into our status of adopted children is to enter into that fullness of life which the Father wishes to confer and Jesus promised in the Father's name. It is to enter into true brotherhood with Christ and thus to stand before the Father in a unique and trusting relationship which can only nurture and deepen that love from which it is sprung. To be content to remain merely "children of Abraham" avails us little. "God is able of these stones to raise up children of Abraham." The fact of our baptism alone is simply not enough to make our adoption significantly more important than a legal fiction. What is asked is this: that we acknowledge the Father's love for us and make it a reality; that we strive with our whole being to live our lives in the light of his love, and thus to return it. The Trinity will come and abide in us with such frequency that soon we can say with ever-increasing truthfulness: "Not my selfishness now, but the love of Christ lives within me." We may then become ever more authentically one with our Father; brothers and sisters of Jesus, and coheirs with him in the Father's kingdom.

As we grow in closeness with God, care must be taken to make our own those values and perspectives which the Father embodies. If this does not happen, if our insights and goals do not reflect those of the Father, our "adoption" will suffer.

Among the attitudes we must watch are those which pertain to suffering, failure and, above all, that false success which we sometimes call "security." Anyone who seriously wants to live as Jesus did will strive to emulate his attitudes.

5

"Where Your Treasure Is . . ."

Man's search for happiness can lead him to take many paths. Some seek it calmly, others desperately. For all of us it is an inescapable quest which comes from the very depths of our nature, one which is part and parcel of the "why" of our very existence. We so thirst for happiness, even where it cannot truly exist; frequently we feel we have found it in security.

In reality, security is very much a double-edged sword. On the one hand, it is necessary for growth and development of both the individual and society, providing the atmosphere, tools and "freedom" necessary for advancement. Great civilizations both past and present, were able to make impressive strides in the arts and sciences only in times of peace and security. The man forced to worry continually about the source of his next meal has little time for "the finer things." Another important aspect of security is that it is an integral part of our God-given thrust. As Theillard de Chardin has said, man is continually striving to return to his point of ultimate security,

God himself. On the other hand, however, the drive for security poses a great danger: that security itself can be viewed as a panacea or universal cure for our ills; it can become an all-consuming obsession — the single goal of all our endeavors. "When I am secure, financially, personally," we say, "then I will have the time and the means to worry about higher things, even my salvation."

We need to read again this parable from the Gospel of Luke: "There once was a rich man who had land which bore good crops. He began to think to himself, 'I do not have a place to keep all my crops. This is what I will do,' said he, 'I will pull down my storehouses and build them bigger. I will collect in them all my corn and other goods, and then say to myself, 'Man, you have plenty of good things laid by, enough for many years: take life easy, eat, drink, and enjoy yourself.'" But God said to him, "You fool, this very night you must surrender your life; you have made your money — who will get it now?" That is how it is with the man who amasses wealth for himself and remains a pauper in the sight of God (Luke 12:16-21). How many people have we known to whom that parable could be applied? To our own peril we forget the fragility and transitory nature of this life. Even in the fulfillment of our personal and financial needs, we are never really secure.

The second danger inherent in our drive to achieve both social and economic well-being is seen in our failure to perceive that the source of all our joy in life can be found only in God — our true security. To the degree that we allow our-selves to equate material success with "total" happiness, we allow security to become our god, to displace the true God in our lives. We are greatly tempted to do just that, but if we make security the object of our worship, then we be-come master of our "god"; we assume the role of "god." We have a concrete example of man's deification of man in the words: "We have no real need of God." The ultimate sociological expres-sion of this line of thought is to be found in the philosophy of Karl Marx: make man materially secure by the communization of goods and ser-vices and he will have no need of God, no use for that opiate which is religion.

This kind of false security need not reside only in the possession of material goods or wealth. It can spring as easily from our tendency toward self-complacency, our inclination to expect that our talents and abilities alone should bring us the happiness and success we seek.

At one time I felt so secure, so confident of my ability that I did not see any real need for God. He was nice to have around sometimes but not really necessary to what I was doing or planning. In fact there were times when God was simply in my way. If I felt any need for God, it was solely to have him put his stamp of approval on what I had already decided should and would be done. Often the contest between my will and God's will was not just a wrestling match, it was all-out warfare and I was determined to be the victor, not the vanquished. My administrative talents, real and imagined, made me very self-assured, very secure. All I really needed was the job before me and myself. I could take charge of all things and manage them quite well. All God had to do was acknowledge the wisdom of my plans and decisions and the power of my efforts, then step out of the way. My prayers often assumed the tone of commands: "Dear God, you had better do this or that because I wish it to be done." I was totally secure, totally sure of myself and of my ability to make things happen my way. I certainly did not feel any real need of God. He was not running my world, I was. As I write this, how embarrassingly childish and silly it all seems now!

Total security is a myth. No man can be so totally self-assured as to be entirely independent, having no need of others, no reliance on anyone, even God. Greater security may make one less dependent, but security can never be great enough to remove all dependence. That is an immense blessing for mankind in general and for each of us individually. People who need people are not only the luckiest people in the world, they are also the richest.

While ample confidence may indeed be necessary for our good, too much emphasis on security has the opposite effect. It stunts our growth. It makes us closed persons: narrow, suspicious, jealous, envious, even ruthlessly ambitious, unable to trust either God or our fellowman. We therefore become psychologically unable to share our time,

41

our talents, our very selves.

Jesus tells us that the meek (the "gentle," the "poor in spirit") will inherit the earth. Perhaps no other teaching is so scorned. It simply does not reflect our experience or philosophy of life. It flies in the face of the great American dream. We have been led to believe that implicit in our acceptance of these words of our Lord is a denial of our very human nature. Too often we reject this teaching through misinterpretation or because we have not bothered to understand it. In our society it is the prosperous, the strong, the powerful who are glorified — not for their personal worth, but because they are rich and influential. The "meek" have no place among us.

Yet it is precisely the meek who inherit this earth and the reason for this is quite obvious. The meek do not allow themselves to be controlled by the desire for material things. The "strong" on the other hand become more and more possessed, "owned," by those very things which are the source of their power and strength: money, position, even "friends." The truly meek inherit the earth while the earth inherits the strong who become slaves to all they have. In this sense, the poor in spirit are genuinely blessed. They alone know how to both make use of the world's resources and avoid being consumed by them.

For the follower of Christ, worldly security must always be kept in proper perspective; not every person is inspired to sell all he has, nor would this be advisable. Many considerations may have to be taken into account in deciding the degree of evangelical poverty one is called to embrace. Every Christian is asked to recognize the mutual need of himself and his neighbor for God and each other, as well as his obligation to meet that need by the sharing of his goods and his time.

Sharing is an integral part of loving which involves the recognition of our basic dependency on and need for one another. Our willingness to share is a measure of our faith in God, of our love and desire to live as Jesus lived. This is what St. James means when he says that faith without good works is lifeless and why he can say with such assurance: "The kind of religion which is without stain or fault in the sight of God our Father is this: to go to the help of orphans and widows in their distress and keep oneself from being possessed by this world" (James 1:27).

St. Paul, who learned everything he knew about Jesus through personal association with him, gives us an excellent rule of thumb for our stance as Christians in this whole matter of security: "Those who deal with this world's goods, should not become absorbed by them." It is a caution we may well heed, containing the true key to happiness both in this world and the next. It is also the one sure antidote to our universal fear of failure.

6

Failure

I said in an earlier chapter that I lived a good part of my life in terror of failure. That fear is still with me but to a much lesser extent. Its effects have been devastating. I am beginning, however, to see that failure need not be the kind of self-destructive force I had always imagined. In reality, dealing properly with failure can assuredly be a gateway to growth, to a new understanding of what is and is not really important in my life. I have found that there exists in fact something far worse than loss of success. One can lack the inner freedom to fail, even to allow oneself to err. The ability to calmly risk failure is a great gift. It can truly liberate me.

I am of course a product of my times and culture. In our society success is everything. From an early age we are *taught,* often in our family circle, that what matters is not effort but success. The question most often asked is not, "How much did you try?" but, "Did you pass?" "Did you win?" It is automatically presumed that if you failed, you simply did not try hard enough. The guilt is yours.

Inevitably and tragically, this "success-conditioning" is linked to our sense of self-worth, our identity. We quickly learn that a very clear pattern dominates our lives: if I win, I'm someone; if I lose, I'm a "nobody," a non-person. The winner always receives the attention, publicity, and promotion. It is never the loser.

All too frequently and still more tragically, this basic pattern is transferred to the area of indepth relationships. Success becomes synonymous with acceptance ("love") by others, especially those whose regard we value most highly. The pattern is the same: success engenders esteem; failure, rejection.

It is hard to exaggerate the frequency of these patterns in our society or the havoc they wreak. We have been so intimidated by the possibility of failure that we will do anything to succeed. No effort is too costly; no price too high; nothing is so sacred that, should the necessity arise, it could not be sacrificed: our health, peace of mind, values, home, marriage, family, friends — all are expendable in our drive to escape failure, to achieve success. Failure, sometimes only apparent failure, must be avoided at all costs. It is the ultimate and often unforgivable sin.

In the light of this, it is not surprising that we should find it difficult to accept the fact that failure, both real and apparent, was part of Jesus' life. After all, Jesus was God! Yet in his life among us, Jesus tasted failure many times. Were it not so, he would have been less than human, not really one of us, not truly like us in all things but sin. Were it not so, we would never have learned the important elements of failure — its acceptability, and role in our spiritual growth.

From the human viewpoint Jesus fails acutely. His life ends in apparent failure. With all his eloquence and example, and with the exception of Nicodemus and Joseph of Arimathea, Jesus fails to reach the Jewish leaders. They reject him from the very beginning. As the time for his Passion nears, even the common people — those who had received so much from Jesus and clung so closely to him — even they leave him in ever-increasing numbers. The closer he comes to the heart of his mission the greater the defections among his most trusted companions until on Calvary we find only his mother, a few women and one disciple. No one else! Even then the world did not like a loser!

One scene from his life highlights Jesus' failure in a particularly poignant way. He had repeatedly and clearly taught his followers that his Kingdom was not of this world. Let us consider this scene in the light of that teaching. The scene takes place at the beginning of those hours in Jesus' life which we have come to call his Passion. It is recorded in chapter 22 of Luke's Gospel.

Jesus' suffering at this point is intense. He already knows, and possibly even feels somewhat, the intolerable agony, the unspeakable suffering

46

and shame he will experience during the next few hours. His heart is heavy with the weight of what is to come and with its overwhelming importance as well. He knows that these short hours are critical in his mission and cannot be avoided. He desperately seeks consolation, support, solace. He returns to his most intimate followers, his closest friends loved so deeply by him and for whom he has done so much. On this, the last night of his earthly life, he wants to be with them alone, to draw strength from their love for him. He still has so much to say to them, to make clear to them. He strongly desires to share this last meal with them. Because it is the Passover Supper, so dramatically symbolic not only of the release of the Jews from bondage but also of the deliverance of man from the slavery of sin to the fullness of redemption, this meal is very special. Here, in the presence of those who are in a unique way the objects of his love, Jesus will do under sign and symbol at this meal the very thing he will physically accomplish on the following day: offer himself up, empty himself totally for them and all mankind. It is impossible to overstate the love and the pain with which Jesus approaches this moment.

The room is prepared. The supper begins. An argument breaks out among the disciples. An altercation, in this scene of such intense love! What do they quarrel about? Their dispute focuses upon who will be the greatest in the Kingdom — the *earthly* kingdom. Surely at that moment Jesus experienced fully and acutely the pain and frustration of failure. After all his teaching, explanation, and example, even his closest companions do not understand. They have not grasped the message!

Jesus' agony of defeat does not end with that incident, painful for him as it must have been. There is no suffering so sharp as that born of rejection by one's most intimate friends. Later during this same meal, Judas will cast Jesus off as a failure. In Judas we have the embodiment of all those who will scorn Jesus, mock him, irrevocably reject him. To save himself, even Peter will doubt, deny and abandon Jesus. Only the insensitive could hold that Jesus felt no pain over all this, that he did not taste here the bitterness of failure.

In his novel *The Adventures of Augie March,* Saul Bellow captures well the "necessity" of failure in Jesus' life: "Well, you understand, everyone has bitterness in his chosen thing. That is what Christ was for, that even God had to have bitterness in his chosen thing if he was really going to be man's God, a God who was human — that was Christ. Other gods poured on the success, knocked you down with their splendor. Those that did not give a damn!" (pp. 290-291). That is the purpose of Jesus' failure. It is meant to inspire us to follow the God who became so fully human.

We need to fail. Even if he succeeds in avoiding his own self-destruction, the man who flees failure, who refuses to accept and acknowledge it in his life has missed so much.

48

It is through failure that the poverty of our own strength and initiative are revealed, and that revelation turns us toward Jesus, the source of our power and peace. Only in failure do we learn best the futility of our attempts to dominate life. It is here that our creaturehood is most vividly brought home to us, here that we can learn at last to call on God in sincerity and truth. Failure does not allow us to disguise our defeat when we sit so crushed, so alone in the midst of our crumbled designs and dreams that Jesus can freely approach us, removing our sense of shame, futility, and rejection. There he can help us build from the shards and pieces of our runaway pride a new and better self.

In itself, defeat is never important although its lesson is. Failure can harden and embitter us, as we become more determined than ever to "succeed" — to prove our wisdom, strength, and power. It can also soften us, creating the fertile soil in which God's truth and love can grow more fruitfully; teaching us that without Jesus we can do nothing. Failure can bring the endless turmoil of insecurity, frustration, and devastating self-deprecation; or it can bring the calm peace and invigorating joy of seeing through events in our lives to the all-loving wisdom of the Father, who never allows anything to befall us which is not in some way for our own good.

My reaction to losing is always of my own making. I can know defeat as men know it, or as Jesus did. In his life, Jesus may feel the pain of failure but he is never crushed by it. He perceives in it a hidden sign of the Father's love. In the strength of my faith I need never despair, for even when totally unsuccessful, I can live confidently in the Father's love for me — that love which increases in my moments of greatest need; I can live as Jesus did. All I need do is pray, humbly and confidently, with Bartimaeus, the blind man: "Lord that I may see" (Mark 10:46-52).

Failure is simply God at work in my soul. As we shall see in the following chapter, God uses all things, even our suffering, and especially this, to create in us the "who" we are lovingly destined to be.

7

God's Handiwork

"For we are God's handiwork, created in Christ Jesus to devote ourselves to the good deeds for which God has designed us" (Ephesians 2:19).

I said earlier that when we love, we enter into a particular kind of relationship, an essential quality of which is a set of definitive and unbreakable commitments to the one loved.

Anybody who dedicates himself wholeheartedly in love to another automatically commits himself, willingly and blindly, to whatever follows. The minute I place on my loyalty a series of reservations, I lessen, even negate, the intrinsic binding force and innate value of the commitment. In marriage, for example, two people are called on to pledge themselves to one another, unconditionally. To give oneself on this deepest level of human love, and to restrict that commitment to the next time one breaks a leg, or has to eat burned bacon is to make a mockery of it and, even more tragically, of the love on which the marriage vows are based. These vows cannot

51

last, as we so unfortunately are beginning to realize with the yearly national increase in the rate of divorce.

My own commitment to God began, sadly enough, as tentative and not without reservations. Many of my reservations at that time did not really become clear to me until much later when I was able to recognize and attempt to deal with them and the powerful hidden force they exerted on my life. I often acted and reacted with behavior not in keeping with my chosen way of life and which I knew was wrong, even personally harmful, but over which I seemed at times to have little or no control. It was a long time before I could even come to grips with this. I was aware of other reservations on my commitment, but would not admit their existence, even to myself. Still others were conscious to me and admitted. The result of all these reservations, known and unknown, was that I did not really make a commitment to God. Instead I struck a bargain. I would give my life to God, but only as long as God continued to fulfill certain definite dreams and expectations. Whether the starting point of my commitment was love tinged with expediency or expediency tinged with love, I am not sure. But I do know that it was the wrong basis on which to dedicate my life to God, and I had to change.

I have come to learn that a life commitment does not have a termination clause. It is not a contract. It is a covenant. Its true basis must always be love. The willingness to endure the pain and suffering it may bring are part and parcel of any covenant relationship. Making the covenant is one thing; living it faithfully is always slightly more difficult.

A true, vital and authentic commitment to God is always one of love. If it is to last and bear fruit, our covenant with the Father must at some point become filled with love — sincere and lasting love. Implicit in such a dedication of oneself is the willingness to accept whatever consequences may arise as a result of having made it. Among other things, love may bring suffering.

To make a commitment to love is to open oneself to suffering. The refusal to accept any possibility of pain such as affectional commitment might involve devitalizes the love upon which it is based, rendering it hollow and incapable of sustaining stress whereupon it falls victim to inconstancy and selfishness. The terms love and "suffer-less" are mutually exclusive. Our world is so loveless because it has fashioned its own definitive description of love and there is no room in that definition for pain. Society scoffs at the value and necessity of suffering as it relates to love and vainly attempts to fill the vacuum with sex and self-interest, calling these "love." Needing to give and receive love, yet unwilling, perhaps unable, to value the suffering involved, the world creates its own love and wonders at its lack of meaning, its emptiness, its frailty. It is a very sorry state indeed.

"God is love," cries St. John. To approach the

53

life of God is to enter into his love. It cannot be otherwise. The man who is afraid or unwilling to love can never be fully Christian. Jesus came to dwell among us as the incarnation of the Father's love, the medium and the message of what union with our Lord means: "The Father and I are one" (John 10:30). In this love, indeed because of this love, Jesus suffered.

At the moment of our rebirth we lovingly committed ourselves to Jesus and became one with him. Joined with him in love, we can expect to be united with him in suffering, even now. Jesus is indeed risen, but his redemptive suffering of this world continues through us, the members of his body. This is why St. Paul could say so confidently: "It is now my happiness to suffer for you. This is my way of helping to complete, in my poor human flesh, the full tale of Christ's sufferings still to be endured, for the sake of his body which is the Church" (Colossians 1:24).

It is precisely this aspect of spiritual and corporal unity which differentiates Christianity from all other religions.

"Christians range themselves with God in this suffering. That is what distinguishes them from the others. As Jesus asked in Gethsemane, 'Could you not watch with me one hour?' That is the exact opposite of what the religious man expects from God. Man is challenged to participate in the sufferings of God at the hands of a godless world. It is not some religious act which makes a Christian what he is, but participation in the suffering of God in the life of the world for the good of the world" (Bonhoeffer: *Letters From Prison,* pp. 122-123).

There is no real answer to the problem of pain and suffering, not even within the context of Christianity. To say men are doomed to distress because of the original sin is much too simplistic and indefensible an answer. When all has been examined we are left still with mystery. The "Why?" of human hardship remains unanswered.

But if there is no complete answer to the problem of pain within Christianity, we may be sure that only through our faith can suffering find its true purpose and dignity. This is why Jesus does not come down from the cross. To do so would be to lie to us, to assert that love can exist without pain, that suffering is a sham and a fiction rather than something indispensible to happiness and ultimate honor. Scripture tells us clearly that it was *necessary* for Christ to suffer. This was the only means by which he could enter his glory.

Until it has been tempered, that is "tried with fire," steel remains unsuited to the many purposes for which it was created. Through the rearrangement of its molecules by the application of intense heat, steel gains the true strength and flexibility of purpose which constitute its value. What the fire is to the metal, suffering is to the human soul. We too must be purified and strengthened; cleansed of our pride, self-centeredness, coldness and indifference if we are to become true lovers after the mind of God, worthy of him, ready to enter his life and our glory. "I am come to kindle fire on the earth" (Luke 12:49). To glow with the purifying and strengthening fire of love we must be willing to undergo the painful realignment of our own "molecular structure," to be tried as gold, by fire.

This "realigning" is crucial to our happiness. Pain is an essential ingredient of our growth which renews us, giving us the strength and flexibility to be what the Father calls us to be: instruments of his true love; his image in our world. Our lives, purified by suffering but not conquered by it, can serve as signs of the transforming power of God's love.

One simple but effective example of this "transforming" power of suffering comes to mind. Not too long ago I gave a retreat to a religious community. Before one of the sessions which dealt with suffering, I went outside for a walk, both to refresh myself and to meditate on the topic. The sunlight was brilliant — so dazzling I could not see clearly and I put on my sunglasses. The result was not only much clearer vision, but a very clear insight. "Sometimes," I thought, "we need to put on dark glasses in order to see clearly. Isn't that one of the values of suffering?"

In spite of all we have said, it is important to remember that suffering in and of itself is not good but evil. To suffer solely for the sake of suffering is the worst form of madness, an insane exercise in futility. On the other hand, to endure pain through efforts to be closer to Jesus; in loving others purely and deeply as he loved; in at-

56

tempting to enter more fully into his life — that is the height of wisdom, not folly. A wisdom the world cannot grasp. Seeing no value or purpose in pain, many have but one response to it: flight. It is the suffering who face life.

In his book, *The Problem of Pain,* C.S. Lewis uses an analogy which helps us to understand the place and purpose of suffering in our lives: "We are, not metaphorically but in very truth, a divine work of art, something that God is making and therefore something with which he will not be satisfied until it has a certain character. Here again we come up against what I have called the 'intolerable compliment.' Over a sketch made idly to amuse a child, an artist may not take much trouble: he may be content to let it go even though it is not exactly what he meant it to be. But over the great picture of his life (his masterwork), the work which he loves, though in a different fashion, as intensely as a man loves a woman or a mother a child — he will take endless trouble — would, doubtless *give* endless trouble to the picture if it were sentient. One can imagine a sentient picture, after being rubbed and scraped and commenced for the tenth time, wishing it were only a thumb-nail sketch whose making was over in a minute. In the same way, it is natural for us to wish that God had designed for us a less glorious and less arduous destiny; but then we are wishing not for more love but for less" (pp. 30-31).

In considering this analogy, and with it the whole problem of suffering, we must be careful to keep a proper perspective. God does not exist for man. We exist so that God may love us. That is our destiny, our highest purpose. For this reason, fleeing all suffering is harmful: it leaves love diminished. "For those whom the Lord loves the same does he reprove, that he may love them the more" (Proverbs 3:12). Our suffering is always a manifestation of God's love for us. Love always demands the perfecting of the loved one. As the letter to the Hebrews puts it:

> "Endure your trials as the discipline of God, who deals with you as sons. For what son is there whom his father does not discipline? If you do not know the discipline of sons, you are not sons but bastards. If we respected our earthly fathers who corrected us, should we not all the more submit to the Father of spirits, and live? They disciplined us as seemed right to them, to prepare us for the short span of mortal life: but God does so for our true profit, that we may share his holiness. At the time it is administered, all discipline seems a cause for grief and not for joy, but later it brings forth the fruit of peace and justice to those who are trained in its school" (Hebrews 12:7-11).

One last caution must be given. In order to see purpose and value in suffering, we must be careful to distinguish between "liking" and "loving." This is a distinction which our society often blurs to its own confusion. Liking asks nothing of the one liked; it is pleased with and accepts him as he is. Also, liking offers no incentive, no challenge to grow, improve or emulate the person liked. Finally, liking carefully tolerates. Loving does not. Loving calls for effort both on the part of the lover and the one loved. Love always evokes a response, whereas liking takes the other where he is and leaves him there. Loving inspires and invites: "Come further; *be* more fully; let your goals become realities." That journey forward always involves pain: spiritual, psychological, and sometimes physical. God does not like us; he loves us. In spite of the pain it may bring, that love is our greatest gift.

No one has known the transforming power of suffering that Jesus experienced which is so clearly illustrated in the Transfiguration. As Jesus stands transfigured on Mount Tabor, resplendent in glory, talking with Moses and Elijah, who were his predecessors, he lives for our instruction, the aftermath of the Calvary which is to come. The message of Tabor is clear: suffering and death will come to him, and they will pass. Jesus will once again be united in the fullness of love with the Father, glorified with that joy and splendor which Jesus shared with him before the world began. Tabor was for us. Jesus did not need the lesson.

If we are truly one with Jesus, we will love him loyally on Calvary, our own calvary, as much as on Tabor. We realize that just as we are requested to bear the "hard things," the difficult and painful moments he asks of us, we too will be called one day to stand on Tabor and experience with him our time of transfiguration. Our tears will not blind us to the light, the hope we have in Jesus. Even in suffering we will know the joy of seeing the Lord's love at work in us and savor the peace and serenity this knowledge can bring.

> *"Hast thou no wound, no mark, no scar?*
> *Then how art thou of Me?*
> *For, as the Master, so shall the servant be.*
> *Pierced are the feet that follow Me*
> *— yet thine are whole.*
> *Can he have followed far*
> *Who has no wound or scar?"*

"Shut out suffering, and you see only one side of this strange and fearful thing, the life of man. Brightness and happiness and rest — that is not life. It is only one side of life. Christ saw both sides" (F.W. Robertson: *Unspoken Sermons*).

8

"Sing to the Lord, for He Is Good"

God is goodness and love in its most awe-somely beautiful and fullest form. Jesus realized this as no one before him had done, revealing through St. Paul the Father's love or "secret purpose":

> ". . . And yet I do speak words of wisdom
> to those who are ripe for it, not a wisdom
> belonging to this passing age, nor to any
> of its governing powers, which are declin-
> ing to their end; I speak God's hidden wis-
> dom, his secret purpose framed from the
> very beginning to bring us to our full
> glory" (1 Corinthians 2:6-8).

It was this "secret wisdom" which sustained and supported Jesus, enabling him to face opposition, disappointments, suffering, and even the apparent futility which plagued his earthly life. Through hidden "wisdom" Jesus drew his inner strength — the "food" which even his closest followers could not conceptualize until Jesus had risen, and in retrospect they came to understand.

Such "secret wisdom" was really very simple: Jesus *knew,* with unshakeable conviction, that the Father *loved* him. In the light of that knowledge, all things were possible, all suffering bearable.

Jesus brought this "secret wisdom" to the world and shared it with humanity. *The Father loves us, too.* That simple message conveys the key to happiness. True contentment, joy in success and peace in failure are experienced only through our willingness to sincerely believe in the Father's love with every fiber of our being.

The realization of God's love will aid us in seeing beyond superficial events to perceive the inner meaning and purpose of our lives. Happenings in our daily routine will no longer appear as isolated moments but rather as integral parts of the Father's plan for us — of our total love story with him.

My own experience has convinced me that we occasionally perceive God's plan in our life-events immediately, i.e., at the time they happen. Not infrequently, however, the "hidden purpose" of life-events is seen only in retrospect. Because of many such instances in my past, I believe that in the perspective of faith, nothing "happens" without God's intention that we or someone else benefit from our encounter. I am quite sure that simply upon reflection, you may recall a past experience which became meaningful to you only very recently.

With the knowledge that he is loved, man can become fully alive. The immediate effect of our interiorization of God's love for us is freedom — the independence gained from faith in his love to be ourselves without fear of rejection; to embrace his will.

Any inability on our part to receive the message of God's love and make it our own is regrettable indeed. How much simpler, more peaceful and happier our lives would be with the realization that Jesus truly loves us as does the Father. Our inability to bring ourselves to believe this must have been Jesus' greatest suffering. It might well have been that the supreme agony of the Passion was the perceived indifference with which so many would view it.

"I have loved you with a never-ending love," says our God. "Even if a mother should abandon her children, yet will I not abandon you" (Isaiah 49:15).

Revelation resounds with the voice of the Father communicating his love to us. Jesus is his final statement (cf. Luke 20:9-16). The lesson has been well taught. It is now ours to learn.

The comprehension of this lesson will undoubtedly involve change. The acquisition of knowledge inevitably affects the behavior of mankind. Understanding God's love will make its own demands on us.

It might be worthwhile to pause here and review some of our previous thoughts.

We may have to revamp our idea of love by extending its definition to include suffering. We perceive that hardship and love are mysteriously intertwined, that suffering can reflect love, concern and caring. For love's sake, we can endure distress willingly. Even that anguish born of hatred and evil can reinforce and strengthen, sometimes even sanctify. There is no instrument which God cannot use for our good, no evil he cannot turn into a blessing. The ugliest human suffering we may be forced to withstand can be providential and a reflection of divine love. God loves us even in the depths of our pain and can bless us even there.

To truly recognize and appreciate our Father's love we must realize that he created us as indeed the crowning glory of that continuing creation which God pronounces "good" and only slightly less spiritually united with him than the angels. How could anyone fail to perceive God's love? He made us loveable. We are after all "flesh of his flesh and blood of his blood," made in his image, his likeness.

God loves us even in spite of our sinfulness. Loving the beautiful or attractive person is never difficult. It takes genuine insight and goodness to see beneath superficialities and love the inner person. It is always the inner person that God knows and loves (cf. Luke 16:15). The Father desires only our happiness, our good. He alone can really read our hearts and is never disturbed or dismayed by that inner poverty which is our essential sinfulness, knowing the truth: that we are always loveable. His everlasting love can never be diminished by our actions. We have only to reach out for it in our lives.

We have already touched on these points, but this kind of fidelity in love is so far removed from our experience that we find it difficult to accept, comprehend or be comfortable with. True loyalty, God's kind of faithfulness, appears increasingly less evident in human relationships, particularly those founded on love. Humanity's love is often characterized by short-term commitments. One can only hope that the self-destructiveness of this reality will soon be recognized and society will move to correct it. Meanwhile, we Christians must realize that the emotions we feel for those who possess our affection should not be confused with our love for the Father. Human relationships, no matter how close, romantic or affectionate, often reveal much that is really foreign to love.

In our sinfulness, which creates no obstacle to his love, we are to the Father what a "wounded" child, one physically or psychologically disabled, is to its parents: an opportunity whereby even greater love can be shown. Every Old Testament analogy describing Israel's relationship with the Father appears as a love image: husband/wife, father/child. Each time Israel sins, one of these examples becomes profoundly significant in the call to conversion. Surely there is a message for us in this.

Finally, in truly understanding God's eternal love for us, we may need to reconsider our fear of loving him too deeply in return. While realizing instinctively the beauty of his love, how powerfully it can inspire, we may fear the possibility of becoming overwhelmed by God and lost to ourselves. We share the anxiety of the poet who fled God "lest having thee, I have naught else besides." The fear of "dying to self" is frequently quite real, even among those who fully comprehend the meaning of that phrase. This fear provokes tension between our conditioned psychological responses and our spiritual desire to answer the Father's call by offering ourselves to him completely, trusting implicitly his love for us. We have been so conditioned to believe in the existence of only that which can be readily apprehended by our senses and therefore has a physical presence or "reality" in our lives that Biblical faith remains difficult for us to attain and its consideration can become anxiety provoking.

It is necessary that we prayerfully meditate upon this tension. Alone, the leap into Biblical faith is an impossibility. The living of our love for God is not possible without God. We must pray for light and strength to overcome the fear of loving God too much, thereby enhancing our ability to act on belief in his love. We need freedom to increase our capacity for complete confidence in God, even though trust in him may seem silly and useless in the light of our existential experience. This "leap of faith" is made possible by a willingness to achieve spiritual death of self so that we may be reborn in love.

To realize our Lord's love and rejoice in it with his Son, we must perceive the Father as Jesus did. How might this be accomplished? By abandoning our pet stereotypes of God: divine policeman, bookkeeper, etc., some of which have remained with us since childhood; by discovering the Father as he truly is rather than as he appears in our fantasy. We must understand that our God in no way resembles man-made deities. Pagan gods are fashioned by men out of need or fear, never love. They are idols of destruction, vengeance, dread. Unlike these alarmingly fanciful images, our God communicates love — he is Love.

"The truth is, I love you," says the Lord. "I am not like other gods — even those you have fashioned for yourselves out of your pride, your undue ambition, your excessive self-love. I do not love you only when you are good, when you succeed, when you do only what I want, when you never sin, when you flatter and appease me by your prayers and sacrifices. *I always love you.* Your 'goodness' does not increase me nor your 'badness' diminish me. Only your love affects me. My love is not born of selfishness. It only seeks what is for your good, my beloved. Everything I do is an expression of my love. I *am* Love. Abide always in my love and you will find rest. That is what I wish for you. It is my greatest gift because in my love I give you myself. All I ask is that you love me in return."

"Father, Lord of heaven and earth, I thank you for hiding these things from the learned and the wise and revealing them to the unlearned. This is how you were pleased to have it be."

9

"When You Pray . . ."

If one is sincerely desirous of drawing closer to the Father in a loving relationship, he will want to pray. Prayer remains the key to growth in love of God. Truly meaningful prayer appears always as an expression of love. Prayer not voicing love degenerates into that meaningless activity so characteristic of pagan worship: empty ritual which leaves no lasting impression, causes no spiritual development. Such "prayer," "full of sound and fury, signifying nothing" has not ever really touched our lives. It was never Jesus' prayer.

Fear of drawing too close to God can keep many at this relatively unsatisfying and fruitless level of devotion. The problem with this "surface" prayer is that even though it accomplishes little, it causes us to believe we are really praying. It brings nothing to that growth, deepening and strengthening of love which should always be the fruit of our prayer. Communicating with God on this level does not lead to a deepening relationship; an ever-increasing knowledge and love of the ME who is known and loved by God, or of the God who loves the ME.

Truly authentic prayer, that contributing most to my growth, always contains the essentials of all productive communication: listening and response. The essence of prayer is communication, a voluntary reaching out to "touch" God. Consciously or not, if in my life I am continually "touching God," then I live in a "state of prayer." I am praying always.

Our concern here includes not primarily the various categories and forms of prayer but rather something of its nature and substance. How might one experience "communication" through prayer?

My best prayer comes when I allow myself to contemplate the presence of God and feel a warmth, and depth of closeness with him. I enter into a profound experience of union with him not in any intellectual or philosophical sense but emotionally, spiritually. During these times, unaffected by any desire, taste or need for words, I approach a kind of dream-like state and feel a heightened awareness. Although I realize this gift is priceless, I also understand that as my encounter with God deepens, he will ask more of me and I risk failing to give of myself completely. In my exhilaration however, I am willing to give my whole being and risk anything for him. I find it impossible to adequately describe these moments which are for me the height of communication with God and the most rewarding times of my life.

True communication demands courage and

humility. To really relate to someone requires that we reveal ourselves openly. Obviously such revelation involves a good deal more than commenting on the weather or one's state of health. In-depth communication is really an exchange of "gifts" wherein I "give" you my "self" in all its truth and nakedness and in return you offer me your "self" through responsive listening and love. It is this in-depth communion which concerns us here.

Requiring great honesty and trust, the communication of "self" does not come easily to us, nor is it ever possible except in an atmosphere of loving acceptance. Objective self-evaluation and confidence enhance our ability to achieve close personal relations through confiding in one another.

Self-acceptance need not imply complacency. There is always need for improvement. A sense of personal worth remains a necessary and critical factor in our development as we struggle to attain our goals, for God does not withhold his love simply because we have not attained the perfection we have the potential to achieve. God loves us in our past, present, and future. His love is eternal; all encompassing.

Trust will always remain essential to in-depth communication. Without this basic confidence of loving acceptance by others no matter what may be revealed about oneself, fruitful communication is impossible. As long as fear of rejection rules me, I speak from behind a mask, unable to give freely of myself. Communication will remain formal, stiff and superficial unless I come out of the dark and let my self be seen. There is a banner in one of the conference rooms where I work which sums up my thoughts so far. It reads: "If I bare myself to you as a person — don't laugh at my nakedness."

Not all interpersonal communication can or should proceed on this in-depth level. There are many instances in our daily living where talking of the weather is more than justified. The person who feels an uncontrollable need to communicate his most personal feelings with everyone and anyone either lacks prudence or requires psychological counseling. But all of us need a "someone" to whom we can confidently bare ourselves with reasonable assurance of understanding and acceptance, a person before whom we may stand openly and without shame, revealing the fullness of our inner poverty, with every confidence of being loved in spite of it all; perhaps more accurately *because* of it all. Once again, every one of us needs a friend.

In an earlier chapter we quoted St. Augustine: "A friend is one who knows all about you and loves you just the same." Surely God is such a person. What is there about our SELF that God does not know? What of our struggles, successes, or failures remains unseen by Him? "Before I formed you in the womb, I knew you." How can we fail to approach with confidence this God who knows and loves us so well? Only pride with fear of rejection stands in our way as was true of Adam and Eve in the garden. Scripture tells us that after having eaten the forbidden fruit, their eyes were opened to their own nakedness which they sought to cover with fig leaves. Later, upon hearing God approaching them in the garden, they hid themselves. Naked, ashamed, and afraid of God's reaction, they hid them-SELVES. Their efforts were futile. God found them just as he finds us in spite of our equally futile efforts to cover our "nakedness" and "hide" from him. When God asks Adam why they hid, Adam replies: "I heard the sound as you were walking in the garden, and I was afraid because I was naked, and I hid myself." God answered: "Who told you you were naked?" God knew Adam's nakedness before Adam did — and it did not repel him (cf. Genesis 3:8-11).

True growth in prayer requires that we conquer our fear of being too close to God, of letting him know us too well. We must compose ourselves, rest peacefully in his love and realize that God always loves us even in the depths of our inner poverty; our need for healing, reassurance, consolation and strengthening. We need not be sinless to pray this way, only truly sorry for our sins.

As our self-perception increases through prayer or true communication with the Father, we clearly view the void which only God can fill, the wounds he alone can heal. Acknowledging our need for true affection, we await the Lord of love who will heal and transform us so that someday we may truly say with St. Paul: "I live, now not I, but Christ lives in me" (Galatians 2:20).

If our prayer does not result in this growth, perhaps we are "saying prayers" and not really praying. Real prayer demands an almost palpable sense of the Father's love for ME. I must become vitally aware that God loves ME. Then I can begin to grow.

Always remember that it is we who need to pray. God wants our prayers. He doesn't need them. Our prayers do not add to God nor does our refusal to pray diminish him. Through prayer we become free, as children of God, to make use of that "hidden knowledge" mentioned by St. Paul (discussed in chapter seven) which allows us to see through our pride and shame. This is why God encourages prayer; it is good for us.

How easily we may be led to believe that people initiate prayer! Authentic prayer is always a response. Sometimes silently, often more perceptibly, God always makes the first move. He invites us to pray, calls us to commune with him. In deciding to pray, we are really responding to his call. Three times each day, the imam calls faithful Moslems to prayer. Whether through the loud voice of such a spiritual leader or the silent urging of our own hearts, the same God continually calls his people to prayer. In our varied response to that call of joy, sorrow, praise, adoration, etc., we make our most fruitful prayer.

It is possible, even necessary, to distinguish

between merely saying prayers and praying. The Our Father, the Rosary and other devotions, the Sunday Liturgy — these are certainly valid forms of prayer. However, when we pray these prayers without any effort to enter into our prayer, without any attempt to identify with the sentiments and the message, we are merely mouthing words, engaging in meaningless activity. And when we merely "say prayers," the Father's remonstration, "This people honors me with their lips, but their hearts are far from me" (Matthew 15:8-9) is well deserved. There must always be something of myself in my prayer or it will be empty prayer.

While pursuing a meaningful communication with God, we must be careful that our prayer does not suffer from a false sense of our personal unworthiness. It is possible to "hide" behind our supposed unworthiness, using it as an excuse for doing little or nothing to further advance ourselves in faith and love. This can become a paralyzing stance, keeping us continually in a state of spiritual childhood. It is not God who finds us unworthy but we ourselves. It is ridiculous to hold that we must "earn" God's love; he loves us freely. Similarly, we do not have to learn to be "good." We *are* good. God made us so. Our actions may be "bad"; *we* are always good — made to the image and likeness of God.

Real prayer stems from and reflects our being, does not require us to step apart from life, casting it aside like some unnecessary burden. Rather we should bring our lives to prayer and our prayer to life. This is the essence of spiritual communication. God does not want only our good news, praise and flattery, he is also pleased when we cry on his shoulder. Our Lord remains unsurpassed in drying tears, calming fears and sharing suffering. He appears never closer to us or more attentive, than when we need him most. To pray with meaning is to stand before God in that truth which reflects myself as I am at the moment of prayer. Even prayers of petition must manifest real needs and genuine awareness of our dependency on God.

Perhaps the following passage will shed additional light on what I have just said. (This excerpt is taken from an article entitled *Knowing Yourself Through Prayer* by Patricia Collins, which appeared on page 236 of the winter 1978 issue of *Spiritual Life*. Miss Collins points out that her article reflects her lived experience of prayer. In part, it reflects mine as well.) "In prayer, which for me often takes a form similar to talking to myself, but with a keen awareness of the presence of God, all one's defenses can be dropped. This is probably the greatest aid there can be in getting to know one's self. When presenting ourselves to others we often (always?) have some awareness of how we are coming off to them. We screen our thoughts, guard our words, struggle to preserve our own image. Many of our reasons for presenting these defenses may be very good. Still the fact that we do incorporate them keeps us from being our true selves, from discovering our real motives, thoughts, feelings.''

Following is a very simple example, which could be duplicated many times from daily life. I was at a meeting and the call went out for a volunteer for a certain unpopular job. There was complete silence as people looked down, around, away. An uncomfortable tenseness filled the room. I ended up volunteering, without giving too much thought to the matter at the time.

As I was driving home I felt vaguely dissatisfied with myself, aggravated that I got into something I now realized I didn't want at all. I asked myself how this happened. I began to relive in my mind the way it had occurred. Thoughts went something like this:

"Well, I volunteered because no one else did. I felt bad for the person asking and I wanted to help out. . . . No, that's not really it. You know what, I think I volunteered at that moment because I felt everyone would be grateful to me. It would take them off the hook, and they'd be thankful. I don't really care about that old committee! I just wanted to look good and reliable when no one else was willing to."

It is in such random, often rambling thoughts that we can get to know our own motives better. In the safety of our own minds, we can come to admit our real motivation, our sincere desires. For there, at least in those few brief moments of reflection, of introspection, we do not have to be concerned with hurting someone else, with preserving how we want others to see us. There we can get at the truth, and decide what we want to do with it.

The process just described may not be prayer, but only a deeper look into one's self which can be beneficial. However, those same thoughts accompanied by an awareness of God's presence, become a prayer, whether we actually preface them with "Dear God" or not. The aforementioned passage is thought-provoking, raising additional considerations such as: "What should I have done, and for what reasons? Where do I go from here?" I now realize more clearly that I should begin to weigh an event not so much in the light of how I look to anyone else, or even to myself, but rather how I look to God as his presence becomes the dominant factor in my thoughts, his will more important than mine.

Nothing in my previous statement is intended to deny that we learn a great deal about ourselves from others. But even here reflection is necessary to reach new awareness. Events we are a part of and feelings aroused in us comprise our thoughts, some of the most significant of which may come in those apparently unimportant moments — riding a bus, walking the dog, sweeping the floor. Prayer, wherein we contemplate relationships with other people, not only enhances awareness of our own thoughts, feelings and desires, but can also help us become more sensitive and responsive to the needs of others.

We must be aware too that God is not interested in bargaining with us. To tell God you will do this if he will do that is not prayer. It is a trade-off. God has no time for games. He will hear our petitions only when they reflect real needs. No matter how well we know our requirements, our Lord knows them better. Trusting in his love and wisdom will bring peace.

Confidence in his Father's love always remains the framework of Jesus' prayer. He lived continually in love with the Father, in obedience to his will. Jesus was continuously about his Father's business, accomplishing the mission entrusted to him. It was from this context, and within it, that our Lord's prayer arose. His hope was always that he might see more clearly and love more deeply in order to fully accomplish the work he had been sent to do. Jesus lived his prayer. If we would live as Jesus did, our prayer must echo his.

To quote again from Miss Collins' article: "It is my experience that the habit of prayer leads not only to better mental health (as one slowly sheds the outer layers of personality that so easily clutter one's life and cloud what really matters), but also to spiritual development. No, I'm not claiming I've achieved any magical inroads to God's will for me or anyone else. But I have become much more aware of His presence in my life, and I do seek a knowledge of His ways, that I might grow in them. I have realized more deeply the effect of my decisions, my words, my actions on others, and I have felt more keenly the Supreme standard against which to measure such things. My life has become more meaningful."

10

Sent Forth

Our commitment to live as Jesus did requires that, in imitation of Christ, we strive to understand and live the Father's love for us in our own lives. This basic commitment is in reality a resolution to grow. When we pledge ourselves in love with the Father, we automatically include as well our willingness to grow in that love. This is the primary focus and aim of our Lord's prayer: "Our Father . . . thy kingdom come." Unless the kingdom "comes" first in us, we cannot contribute to its growth in others. This basic fact is so often overlooked. Our prayer, suffering, etc., must contribute not simply to our own spiritual development but also to the growth of others.

"The kingdom of God is within you." Our efforts to strengthen and advance his kingdom within us must begin with ourselves, both as individuals and as part of a Christian community. Our first "weapon" in this struggle is in meaningful prayer through which we come to know the Father and his love for us. We thereby come to know ourselves as well, learning what help we need to fulfill our mission.

The kingdom will take root in us when we have come to know the Father through prayer, allowing his love to increasingly transform us into his image. The soil in which the kingdom-seed is planted is our faith. In knowing and loving the Father, we prepare for that dedication of self to God which is the beginning of his reign in our lives. Without this leap into faith, only three choices are open to us: we can ignore God; we can live on the periphery of the kingdom; we can try to establish the kingdom by our own efforts and thereby court disaster. Until we enter his kingdom by way of our own deeply committed personal faith, we cannot truly be part of it.

Unless we nurture the kingdom within us by genuine prayer, it will never grow. This is what our Lord tells us in the Parable of the Sower. If our hearts are hard, stony; if we are filled with cares about this life and riches; if our true "god" is security; if our love of the Father is weak and selfish, we cannot receive the seed which is the word of God; it cannot take root in us (cf. Matthew 13:10-23). Only that prayer which sincerely invites the Father to enter our lives can prepare us to receive his word. And only prayer which tells God we love, need and want him can tend the seed of his word and encourage its growth. Only in this way will the kingdom be truly the kingdom of God and not one of our design.

There is no point in strengthening and advancing the kingdom, unless it is truly God's. To attempt to operate independently of the Father would not only be futile but would also indicate a complete lack of understanding regarding the nature and content of the call we have been given.

This essential, most basic call common to all men is simply this: to live out in our lives our love for the Father. Before being summoned to any particular vocation or specific lifestyle, we are called to become extensions of God's love. Our vocation is simply the necessary framework within which we live out this call. In our individuality and uniqueness, we are called to be messengers of the Lord, his ambassadors. This is why it is vital that our mission remain truly God-based. I cannot appear as an extension of his love if God is not within me nor can I preach the love of Jesus if I refuse to hear him. I can never become truly an ambassador if the message I give is simply my own.

Frequently we are blinded by our "success" conditioning. I conversed recently with a fine young man who is a medical student. He told me that his first in-depth contact with terminally ill patients was a very traumatic experience for him. Trained to be absolutely confident in the healing power of his own skills, he had not really been prepared to deal with the incurable. His initial meetings with these people proved quite fruitful, however, causing him to stop and evaluate his chosen profession from a new perspective. This was good. In view of the fact that it afforded him an opportunity to look upon medicine not only as a career, but also as an area for self-dedication, his vision of "success" could be greatly broadened. Moreover, the situation provided a great chance to see his profession clearly in terms of Christian ministry — ministering to the incurable in Jesus' name, not for personal gain or satisfaction — a view he could expand to include his total professional and private life.

I believe that view of work and ministry is open to all of us. We are called to build up, create, and redeem the world — the world of our personal lives, our family life, society. Everyone's occupation somehow contributes to the ease, security, advancement, and health of others. Our daily chores can cease being simply work and become effective Christian ministry arising not from "what" we do, but rather "why?"

The role of parents remains a vital part of the Christian ministry and mission. Not only should Christians be "good" parents in the accepted use of that term; through a deep understanding of their hidden role, they must strive to be better parents to make it possible for the children they nurture to discern in their behavior the values, beliefs and outlook which are Christ's. The image of Jesus which parents convey to their children will make the deepest impression on them. More than all others, Christian parents must stand out in the lives of their children as the ambassadors of Jesus. Theirs is a difficult and demanding role.

An ambassador stands before others, not in his

own name, but as the very personification of the one who sent him. We must ourselves be convinced of God's goodness and love before effectively conveying these to another, find in our own lives the serene peace and joy of life in our Father, before sharing it with others. True missionaries live their faith and prayer. Never let it be said of us that people cannot hear our words because what we are shouts too loudly. Jesus was sent forth as the Father's perfect ambassador, ("The Father and I are one"); so now we are called to represent Jesus, and through him, the Father, to our world. If people do not find Christ in *us* who claim to be his followers, they may perhaps never find him. If we refuse his call through indifference, laziness, selfishness, lack of love and compassion, those to whom we should have ministered in his name will weigh heavily on our consciences.

In our work to enhance the growth of his kingdom, patience with ourselves and God is essential. Through God alone can our mission prove fruitful and he will not be hurried.

Patience does not come easily to us. We are all possessed of a certain natural impatience, heavily reinforced by our culture. Even prayers for patience are sometimes impatient: reflective of our conditioned tendency to expect immediate results. "Dear God, give me patience," we pray, "now." The extent of our impatience should not come as a surprise. We live in an age of "instants": instant coffee, tea, soup, pain relievers, even relatively instant "solutions" to the most complicated life-problems; all aggrandized by television and other media. The magic word of our era is: Now! Impatient with both past and future, we are urged to live for today, so conditioned that these "instants" translate, in our minds, into immediate comfort, security, happiness. Such qualities of being are what the instant advertisements are designed to sell.

All of this psychological conditioning has resulted in a serious reduction of our "patience level." As members of a hyper-impatient society, no longer taking time to distinguish between "want" and "need," we desire instant satisfaction, regardless of the cost. Psychologically, this extreme impatience reduces us to children, unable to wait calmly with faith, easily frustrated, lacking in perseverance, and angry. If our efforts do not achieve immediate results, they are hurriedly abandoned in favor of something that looks more promising. Impatience is a serious deficiency, robbing us of our adulthood, rendering us vulnerable to depression, despair, a growing lack of satisfaction with ourselves, our efforts, perhaps even our lives.

Perfection is certainly a desirable goal. "Instant perfection" however, simply does not exist. Excessive impatience remains one of the less desirable side-effects of our western technology. Only awareness of the existence and subtlety of its impact will prevent impatience from robbing us of peace, interferring with our mission.

The undesirable qualities of this conditioned restlessness spill over into our spiritual lives in many ways. "Why should I continue to pray? Why keep on striving to live in union with God?" we ask. "Nothing has changed. I am not a better person, nor have I overcome this fault or that sin. My situation has neither changed nor improved. The world is not a better place — why should I continue? Why not give up and try something else?"

Allowing a conditioned intolerance of delay to dominate our spiritual lives, we run a grave risk. By tending to rush in and make things happen, we risk ignoring God's will for our own. He wishes that we patiently, calmly and faithfully listen and await him. In our impatient inclination to usurp God's place in the order of events, we embark on a dangerous course.

In all things, God remains the First Mover. When we expropriate the role of creator, then that which we produce comes not from God, but from us who are guilty of building on sand. This thought will be dealt with more fully in a later chapter.

The point here is that there is no room for undue impatience in our spiritual lives. To fruitfully live our basic vocation we must remember that God acts in us; without him we can do nothing of real and lasting value. God never acts until the appropriate time has come, wherein all things are born and come to be, each in its proper order. Jesus is forever the vine and we the branches. By forgetting ourselves and neglecting God, we will not persevere in our call to help spread the kingdom.

Whether self-inflicted, directed at God, or neighbor, man's impatience can never work God's will or diminish him. To truly be ambassadors we must persevere in patience.

Having acquired, through prayer and self-discipline, the patience needed for successfully living our call, we need to pray for strength. Our mission: to give the world a meaningful impression of God is a difficult one. Our Lord had to face grave and discouraging hardship in his discharge of this same mission. Knowing the problems we face, he warned us about them. "If the world hates you, remember that it hated me before you. Do not be surprised if the world hates you. If you were of this world, then the world would love you. But I have taken you from the world, therefore the world will hate you" (John 15:18-19).

The cost of true discipleship is often great. It can even require a willingness to lay down ones life for another. It always requires that we dare to be different. If we truly love the world, a willingness to confront it, to risk the misunderstanding and rejection of others, even our loved one's, can wound deeply and painfully, given our basic need for acceptance. Finding Jesus in the rejection we feel will help us persevere. To stand before our world in a unique way, wherein we may guide others to God — the eternal and certain source of all true happiness, joy, security and peace; to live as Jesus did, as the prophets before him, will bring us the happy fulfillment found in answering his call.

In following Jesus, to all, including our fellow Christians, we must be a support and example, a bulwark of faith and love. We are called, each in his own life, to grow in love toward the fullness of our humanity, the crowning glory of God. Having received life, enlightenment, strength and love from God, we are asked to share these gifts with our neighbors. In this way we will answer our call and Jesus will work in and through us to continue his mission, even to the end of time.

"Go forth therefore and make all nations my disciples — and be assured, I am with you always, to the very end of time" (Matthew 28:19-20).

"You are a letter from Christ . . . . : a letter written not with ink but with the living Spirit of God, written not on stone tablets but on the pages of the human heart" (2 Corinthians 3:3).

11

"Walk in the Light . . ."

By ridding our lives of sin, we establish contact with the Father and fulfill our mission. It is impossible to simultaneously live for the Lord and sin. "You cannot serve God and Mammon" (Matthew 6:24).

Sin and grace are both manifestations of love; the one of self, the other of God. Sin results from excessive self-love, seeking to displace God as the center of my universe and replace him with me. Born of pride, destroying true love and the very self from which it springs, sin prevents growth and leads one to seek his own will at any cost. Its fruit is death.

Paradoxically, promising all, sin robs us of everything. The love of self from which it springs becomes self-contempt. With the loss of love, hate grows. Our self-esteem fades and life appears empty. Sensing the frustration and hopelessness of sin, we feel trapped, isolated, lonely.

"They know God, but they do not give
him the honor that belongs to him, nor do
they thank him. Instead their thoughts

88

have become complete nonsense and their empty minds are filled with darkness. They say they are wise, but they are fools. They exchange the truth about God for a lie; they worship and serve what God has created, instead of the Creator himself. Because they do this, God has given them over to every passion, every foolishness and insanity" (Romans 1:21-22, 26).

Left to ourselves, that is our lot. Our natural innate tendency to sin remains the primary source of our tension, that state of inner conflict between good and evil. Because of our desire for goodness in spite of selfish inclinations, this tension within the conscience generates great agony. To experience peace, we must find forgiveness or somehow justify our sinning. We cannot ignore it.

Left to ourselves our lot is hopeless. But we have been delivered from our sorry state. In the love and Sacrifice of Jesus, forgiveness and reconciliation become ours. We need no longer be slaves of our sinning, desperation and despair. Sin walks in darkness, but God gave us the power to break through the darkness into light, living a new and renewed life as the adopted children of him who we can now call: "Abba, Father."

All true love is "ecstatic" bringing us out of ourselves to become one with our love. We live in our love whether it be money, friends or God. The more my love grows, the more I will die to self in order to be one with the object of my love. This is why Jesus possessed no sin. Sin cannot cohabit with perfect love. When one dwells, as he did, united with the Father through love, there is no room for sin.

The great Christian saints all knew something of the intensity and fullness of love; their smallest sin brought as much agony as their greatest. Both interferred with that total union for which their intense love of the Father caused them to long so greatly. For them, sins differed only in the degree of havoc they played with the love relationship.

We can relate to this attitude. The more we love someone, the more easily we are hurt; the less intense our love, the less easily we are offended. Our will to sin is often influenced by a lack of appreciation of God's longing for our love.

Bishop Fulton Sheen tells of going to confession on one occasion and having the priest ask him whether he thought that what he confessed had been a mortal sin or not. The Bishop replied: "Father, I don't know and I don't care. All I know is that I hurt the Lord and I don't want to ever do that." There is a great lesson in his answer. Its love leaves no room for baseless fear.

At one time or another, I have felt the fear of acknowledging sin; I have known the gnawing doubt of the Father's forgiveness in my heart. Pride and shame have overwhelmed my love, keeping me a slave to sin. How little we understand the Father's forgiveness revealed by Jesus in the Scriptures! If only we would let go, in total trust; escape the bonds of fear, and run to love. Only God can set us free, for having made the leap into his arms, we wonder at the foolishness of our fear. "You shall know the truth and the truth shall make you free."

Our sin is always before us; we must be ready to confront it. If the just man, the person of great righteousness (the "saint"), can fall seven times a day, we can expect to do no less. The Christian response to failing is not despair but hope, even joy. Love does not preclude sin but rather, forgives it; does not demand perfection but inspires it. It is always the sin, the evil act, which is detested, never the sinner. "Hate the sin but love the sinner" is a philosophy lived sometimes by us, but always by God. "I do not desire the death of the sinner but that he be converted and live," says God. In this aspect of love — its willing forgiveness — our hope lies. Here too we find cause for joy. Repentance can only strengthen us.

Failing to understand that God's forgiveness is constant, permanent, and assured, we lack appreciation of his love. God's love and forgiveness transcend our own. If we lack forgiveness it is not God but we who refuse to forgive ourselves; to enter the Father's arms and repose in his gentle embrace.

How weak faith impairs our trust! We think of God as loving us only when we are "good." We degrade his love. Parents do not truly love their children only when they are "good." Certainly, the evil deeds of children may affect parental love. Human affection always runs the risk of hurt, disappointment, diminution. But if the love is deep and true, the one loved never becomes rejected entirely.

With God, the person is never rejected at all. God always loves us. Our sin does not diminish the Father's love for us. It intensifies it. This is the lesson of the prodigal son. The faithful son remains greatly disturbed by the intense affection and honor with which his father greets his profligate brother. The prodigal son receives more intense love from his father, whom he had so greatly hurt but whose joy is now so full that the sinner becomes an honored guest. It almost seems that the father now loves his son more than he would have had the son not sinned, even though obviously the father would have been happier if his wayward son had never known the pain of wrongdoing. But the son's failure allows the father to show him love with greater intensity, not less.

God never forgives grudgingly. "There is more joy in heaven over one sinner who repents than over ninety-nine just who have no need of repentance" (Matthew 18:13).

Our sinfulness should never stand between ourselves and God, never lead us to despair; for as we repent, detesting our sin rather than ourselves, we experience deeper love.

Repentance and forgiveness are always healing, freeing acts. Jesus said of Mary Magdalene: ". . . Her great love proves that her many sins have been forgiven; where little has been forgiven, little love has been shown" (Luke 7:47). Because Mary has been forgiven, freed from her burden of sin, she can show great love. Surely the same is true of us. Remaining in sin, we choose to block union with God in that very depth of our being where love of the Father should be most active. Sinning hinders unnecessarily our efforts to live as Jesus did. If we do not accept forgiveness or love, how can we forgive, love, or live as Jesus did?

The other side of forgiveness will be the subject of the following chapter.

12

"As You Forgive Us"

If I expect God's forgiveness, I must be forgiving. Forgiving is yet another facet of my total commitment to live as Jesus did by loving as Jesus did.

There can be many possible reasons why I should forgive those who wrong me. It may be to my advantage: the one who offended me may be my boss or someone whose cooperation is necessary to me. I might feel obligated to forgive my offenders: perhaps they have forgiven me many times and simple justice demands that I forgive in return. If the person who offends is a friend, I may forgive out of love.

For those attempting to live their lives in Jesus, forgiveness of others will always be primarily a matter of love. Other motives may enter in, but will remain purely incidental to the real one: love. God will forgive us as we forgive others. "If you forgive others the wrongs they have done, your heavenly Father will also forgive you; but if you do not forgive others, then the wrongs you have done will not be forgiven by your Father" (Matthew 6:14-15). Human and divine forgiveness are inextricably intertwined because love is one. True love can never be divided. "If a man says 'I love God' while hating his brother, he is a liar. For he cannot love God whom he has not seen if he does not love his brother whom he has seen. This is the command Christ has given us: that he who loves God must also love his brother" (1 John 4:19-21).

Unless the love I feel for God and my brother be one and the same, it is not Christian love.

As a Christian, I love my neighbor not because he exists, is loveable or because humanitarian considerations dictate that I love him, but for the simple reason that he is my brother and beloved by the Father. In Jesus, we are one. The powerful and beautiful "oneness" in Christian love reveals the Trinity to all men. "Everyone who believes that Jesus is the Christ, is a child of God, and to love the parent means to love the child; it follows then that when we love God and follow his commands we love his children too" (1 John 5:1-2).

By these words, John does not exclude unbelievers as recipients of God's love or ours. He simply pursues a point which is well taken: to live in God's love, we must be prepared to love as he does. I strive to impart the vastness of the Father's love for me, the depth and beauty of its forgiving quality, to my brother. I can reflect the Father's love in my willingness to forgive fully. Only then will my love be truly "divine."

When I refuse to communicate the forgiving

love God gave me to others, I render it selfish. By not sharing his gift, I deny others that forgiveness which I request of God, perhaps even demand, in the name of that one love which he has for us all. "In the measure that you give, it will be given to you," says Jesus (Matthew 7:2). Surely he means that the love and forgiveness I give others will come back to me.

Much of Jesus' rejection of phariseeism is based on this principle, also the underlying thought of several of the parables (cf. Luke 12:41-46; Matthew 18:23-25). Highlighted by the fact that the only petition of the "Our Father" in any way qualified is that dealing with forgiveness, Jesus' words hold great meaning for us. We pray to be forgiven as we are willing to forgive, communicating God's love. For the Christian, forgiveness remains first and foremost a matter of loving one another because the Father has loved us first.

It follows that our forgiveness cannot be qualified or subjected to self-imposed limitations and conditions. We can never honestly say: "I will forgive you only if you will do such and such"; or "I will forgive you if and when you ask for it." That would not be forgiving with the Father's love. God always forgives; his only prerequisite is our sorrow. Freely given, the Lord's forgiveness does not come to us only upon request. It is always there.

If we are truly of God, our forgiveness will be freely available to others; they will not even have to ask for it because it is a part of our love for them. "Freely have you been given, freely give" (Matthew 10:8). That is the sole guideline for forgiving.

The living out of Christian forgiveness may well require considerable strength of character and self-control in emotional responses to certain persons and situations. We are too easily and quickly hurt.

Overwhelming feelings of anger and disappointment may render us incapable of forgiving. In some people this response becomes extreme and they require professional help to control it. In varying degrees, however, it can be present in all of us from time to time. Care must be taken never to let our negative emotional responses so possess and "harden" us that we lose our capacity for Christian forgiveness.

Effective handling of this problem demands that we show greater perceptivity, avoid coloring the actions of others with our own motivations and refrain from judging, especially too quickly and rashly. Self-pity, narrowness and false pride should never be allowed to gain mastery over us.

Not free simply to ignore or tolerate this damaging lack of emotional control, we must work to correct it before we are rendered incapable of forgiveness. Unchecked it can often destroy love and foster hatred.

In refusing to deal with our negative feelings, we suffer. Bitterness and a longing for revenge only breed unhappiness and self-destruction.

I once met a young man who had suffered deep rejection and misunderstanding. Raised on a farm and made to feel he was simply one more mouth to feed and one more hand to work, his whole attitude was: "I've been used long enough. It's time I started using others." As soon as he was able, he ran away to the city. Soon this frame of mind, coupled with his defensiveness and short temper, began causing him serious trouble. Much later he realized that forgiveness of his parents was vital to his growth, well-being and happiness. After a sincere effort to understand what lay behind their actions, he honestly forgave his parents, even though he could never condone their treatment of him. He subsequently enjoyed a freer, happier, more adjusted life.

Our greatest defense against letting circumstances adversely affect our emotions and attitudes is the gift of understanding, the grace to see the person behind the act; to perceive why it happened. Such comprehension may not lessen our hurt or difficulty even in forgiving the actual offense. But it should make possible and easier forgiveness of the person behind the offense.

There is a reason behind every human action. The explanation may be obvious or subtle, conscious or unconscious, revealed or hidden. Sometimes one's reasoning may be so warped and twisted as to render it entirely unworthy of approval or acceptance. Whatever the motivation, it will always ultimately arise from the person.

No person's actions are totally unaffected by

the circumstances of his heredity and environment, nor independent of the influences which shape and mold all our lives in varying degrees. The ravings of a madman will always be mad, incomprehensible to those of us who are sane. To him, however, they are perfectly sensible and justifiable. Although our understanding of this man's reasoning will not make his actions any more acceptable, it can, however, make forgiveness of him more feasible if not easier, because of the clarity with which we see the person. We are required to understand and forgive the sinner, but never to tolerate or condone the sin. Rather, God calls us to accept, in love, the sinner.

While the example of the madman appears extreme, this same principle of prayerful understanding applies as well to human activity of a more normal and ordinary nature. The boorish, impolite, temperamental person may be so because he is worried, in pain or basically insecure. The man who treats us with suspicion and dislike may be under a misapprehension about us or something we have said or done. Perhaps another individual suffers because of hereditary or environmental factors. His disposition may be such that he finds life difficult and human relationships a problem. He could also possess great hostility because he is not of God. Sometimes the key to forgiveness consists simply of placing oneself in another's shoes.

A sincere effort to objectively evaluate a situation with a minimum of self-interest and a good deal of honesty, will often enhance our ability to forgive. After considering the ways in which I too might have been or certainly was at fault, I become much more understanding and forgiving.

Whatever the reason, whether the problem resides in us or the one who has provoked our anger, understanding will make forgiveness incredibly easier, perhaps even possible where before it was inconceivable.

A willingness to forget characterizes true forgiveness. What more obvious refusal to forgive can be imagined than the words: "I will forgive but I will never forget"? That attitude only mocks the love from which authentic forgiveness springs. It renders that love hypocritical, unworthy of us or the Father. Such a state of mind does not mirror the love and forgiveness God has inspired. It speaks of human vindictiveness rather than divine compassion and is unjustifiable within the context of Christian love. If we cannot forget we cannot forgive. It is as simple as that! The pain we feel may linger because we cannot control it, but that which caused our pain must be put away. We should pray for the gift of forgetting, the healing, not only of our pain, but our memory as well.

In examining our forgiveness of others, how can we fail to recognize that one significant "other" whose closeness so often tends to be overlooked. I am speaking of our "other self."

It is possible to conceive of ourselves as being two "selves," as it were. St. Paul alludes to this

concept when he writes: "I do not even acknowledge my act as mine, for what I do is not that
which I want to do, but what I detest — for
though the will to do good is there, the deed is
not. The good which I want to do, I fail to do; but
what I do is the wrong which is against my will"
(Romans 7:14-20).

We are often engaged in the same conflict
wherein the other self, whom we might even detest, gains the upper hand as our struggle
becomes lost.

On failing to resist temptation, we must be
careful to make that "self" the object of our forgiving. This is not rationalization but simply
necessary forgiveness. It is impossible to love my
neighbor as myself unless my love includes even
that "self" which although mine, I find to be
unruly, rebellious, even destructive. In not loving
that "self," forgiving it, helping it improve, I
become a divided house, unable to stand.

If I am unable to see myself as loveable in spite
of all my weaknesses and defects, my faith, trust,
joy and peace in God's love for me will be lost.

Here again, prayer remains our most effective
tool. It is important that we ask God's help to heal
our wounded pride, disappointed ambition, lack
of loving.

The residual memory of our own past sin
should never prevent us from loving ourselves. It
is helpful that our sins are always before us, not
as the cause of undue worry, despondency or
despair, but because by remembering them, we

may learn to avoid repeating them. There is truth in the remark made by Santayanna: "He who forgets his past is doomed to repeat it."

In my efforts to love and forgive my neighbor, I must never forget that one "neighbor" who is closer to me than any other — my rebellious and sometimes unattractive self. If I would live as Jesus did, I must forgive and heal as he did.

Each time I effectively forgive, I "die" a little to myself. As we shall see, this death of self is the true vehicle to life in Jesus. Everything spoken of thus far is a prelude to our continuing death and resurrection — our ongoing "rebirth" in God.

13

"Our Death and Resurrection"

One of the less desirable trends in our faith-teaching has been the tendency to consistently interpret the phrase "life after death" too literally. We have come to understand the words "life" and "death" as referring simply to our physical death and the "eternal" or "after" life which will follow that moment in our personal histories. While essentially true, this interpretation is too narrow. It does not capture the fullness of the Christian message. Divorced as it is from daily life and the commitment made at the moment of our rebirth, it cannot lead us effectively to live as Jesus did.

St. Paul places the "death event" not at the end of our life in faith, but at its very beginning: "For you who have been baptized in Christ Jesus, have also died in Him." Jesus himself insisted on the death-rebirth cycle, not in reference to physical death and future existence, but as an absolute condition of our life in him here and now. One who truly follows Christ is never a man simply waiting to die. He is consistently and continually "a dying man."

The preface of the *Liturgy for the Dead* describes very accurately the effect of physical death on our lives: "For your faithful people, life is changed, not ended." Our "eternal" life in the Lord does not begin after our physical death — it simply continues, changed only in the degree of perfection and intensity with which we will then live it. The Christian is inspired to see physical death as symbolic: a real, external and vivid sign reflecting the ongoing dynamic of his whole life, simply an outward manifestation of that continuous interior dying to self and rising anew in Jesus, which is the heart of the Christian call and our source of greatest peace and happiness.

Although I am still frightened by thoughts of death, suffering, failure and sin, such strong signs of our mortality, my reflections on dying are never morbid; I am by nature a very happy person. Perhaps that is the reason a following chapter will center on joy. It seemed natural to me to include that topic. Joy is always the fruit of Christian hope — and Christian "death."

As difficult as it is for me to reflect seriously on death, I always find it extremely helpful to do so.

Facing death, even thinking of it, always clarifies life, reduces events to their basic and inherent simplicity, puts importance in perspective and helps us more clearly penetrate inner meanings and values. Paradoxically, in facing death, we truly find life, whether we are speaking of

104

physical death or of that more important "other death" to self, through which we are reborn.

In Christian faith, therefore, "death" appears as not merely that physical moment we all must face, but also as an integral inseparable component of that mystery central to all authentic life in Jesus which we have come to call the Paschal Mystery. Genuine life in Christ demands the day-to-day living of this Mystery, which happens at the very moment of our free and total commitment to Jesus. Through this mystery we apprehend and experience the essence of the Christian message on life and death.

Within the context of the Paschal Mystery, death is always a prelude to and an absolute condition for life. "Unless the grain of wheat falls to the ground and dies it remains a single grain of wheat. But if it dies it will bring forth fruit in abundance" (John 12:24). To live the Paschal Mystery means then, to reenact in our lives that cycle of suffering, dying and rebirth reflected so vividly in the historic Life, Passion, Death and Resurrection of Christ.

The Paschal Mystery has death as its first component. Implicit in willingly living this Mystery is the acceptance of that suffering which God deems beneficial. To experience it means to suffer the "death" of everything that blocks the growth of God's love in me: my inordinate ambition, self-centeredness, blindness, indifference and coldness — all that would replace Jesus as the true center of my existence. It is that death to self which alone frees my love and enables me to live, in all its newness and fullness, that real life which is mine — a life of love in Jesus. This will involve pain. Suffering is essential to all growth.

One must constantly keep in mind, however, that the thrust and ultimate goal of this "suffering and death" — is new life. The winter "death" of nature rids it of whatever hinders growth, allowing it to gather strength, so that it may burst forth with new life (renewed life) in spring. In the same way, Easter follows Lent. The celebration of triumph and joy, the "Alleluia," resounds in spring when the song of suffering and sorrow has ended and the long night of winter has passed.

In each phase of our new life we are ourselves transformed. The Christ of the Resurrection is the same Jesus of Calvary. But how gloriously transformed! Each time we allow ourselves to follow the suffering-death-resurrection sequence, we approach the very heart of life, living more and more as Jesus did.

In our experiencing of the Paschal Mystery, it becomes essential that we remember that it is always Jesus who gives meaning, purpose and value to our suffering. Through him we are reborn. Our objective remains that greater happiness to which he calls us; the heart of our resurrection. Our Paschal Mystery is never without purpose. Our pain will always be inexorably united with the suffering of Jesus, just as our death and resurrection become one with his. "At all times we carry in our mortal bodies the death of Jesus, so that his life also may be seen in our bodies" (2 Corinthians 4:10).

To be totally fruitful, the vision of our personal and unique Paschal Mystery must include a clear understanding of ourselves as members of Christ's Mystical Body. There is a clear link between the quotation from Paul cited above and the passage in his first letter to the Corinthians in which Paul describes the Christian community, the church, as the Body of Christ (cf. 1 Corinthians 12:12-27). In a vision of life which has endured, Paul saw the Christian community as Jesus living on in his members and, through us individually and collectively, continuing and completing his work of redeeming all men. To paraphrase Paul, we are called to be Jesus in our world. Not Jesus in some vague, ineffectual and almost unrecognizable way — but clearly and unmistakably Jesus: living as he did; making known to our world the love, power and fidelity of the Father; continuing the saving work of that Paschal Mystery which we are all called to share, each in his own way. When Paul later boasts that he makes up in his own flesh those things that are still lacking to the sufferings of Christ, he is referring directly to the living out, in his own life, of the saving Passion, Death and Resurrection of the Lord. He adds that he does this "for the sake of his (Jesus') body, which is the church" (cf. Colossians 1:24), and clearly sees himself as the personification of Jesus to those to whom the Lord sends him: "Be imitators of me as I am of Christ" (1 Corinthians 11:1). Paul is Christ's ambassador. His mission is Jesus'.

We are called to the same mission. Our task involves allowing the Father's love to so transform our lives that we become in a real way that which Jesus was, the incarnate love of God present in our world. Our calling is to give to all life ourselves transformed by love, as Jesus was. How can this transformation be possible unless we live out our unique share of the Paschal Mystery, in imitation of Christ. If humanity is unable to find Jesus in us, it runs the grave risk of not finding him anywhere. As Fulton Sheen has said: "The only argument the world will listen to now is the argument of personal holiness. It has heard all the rest and rejected them" (Sheen: *Retreat to Priests,* Washington, D.C., p. 19).

There is nothing "unnatural" in our living of the Paschal Mystery. In her best-selling book, *Passages,* Gail Sheehy writes: "We are not unlike a particularly hardy crustacean. The lobster grows by developing and shedding a series of hard, protective shells. Each time it expands from within, the confining shell must be sloughed off.

"With each passage from one stage of human growth to the next we, too, must shed a protective structure. We are left exposed, and vulnerable — but also yeasty and embryonic again, capable of stretching in ways we hadn't known before" *(Passages:* Sheehy, Bantam Books, 1977, p. 29).

As persons, we are one: a unit, a "whole." What is true of us psychologically can find easy parallel in our spiritual life. Our inner life must also be a series of passages through which to grow spiritually or we will atrophy. Growth in understanding of self and God is essential. All life demands a series of willing passages. The butterfly cannot exist until the larva has passed. Our innate and intense longing to exist only in love will be fully satisfied when free of self, we rest firmly and eternally in that tremendous Lover by whom, for whom and in whom we have our being. As St. Augustine said: "Our hearts were made for thee, O God, and they shall restless be until they rest in thee." Our journey back to the Father begins not with death but with our birth. It is a journey of the living, not the dead.

Each state of our journey, each transforming phase of our lived Paschal Mystery, brings us as its aftermath something of the glory of Mount Tabor where the transfiguration of our Lord took place as a prelude to his Calvary. There is this difference. For us, "Tabor" must always follow our "Calvary." It can never precede it.

For us as for Jesus, Tabor and Calvary are inextricably intertwined. Both remain necessary, both must be shared, and are for "the good of all." In particular the joy, peace, and "glory" of our Tabors must be shared. During each experience of standing with Jesus on the mountaintop, we enjoy the fruit of our Paschal Mystery — resurrection to new life in him. Glowing with radiance, from each of these mountaintops our light must go forth, to shine before all men that they also may give glory to our Father in heaven.

14

Food for Life

"For it is God himself who works in us both to will and to accomplish all we do" (Philippians 2:13).

In this and similar passages (cf. Ephesians 2:6-10) St. Paul communicates a very basic truth regarding our spiritual life in Jesus. It is, in fact, so fundamental a principle that we continually run the risk of overlooking it in our quest for closer identification with God. This truth is not well received in our technology-minded, activity-oriented society. Technology tends to delude man into believing he can replace God. It does not allow for anything which tends to place man in the created order.

The basic principle of which Paul writes is simply this: In his inner life with Christ Jesus, that existence hidden in God, man's proper role is one of "active-passivity." By this I mean that his part in the life of the Spirit is primarily one of receptivity. In every meaningful spiritual contact, it is God who makes the first move. Man's primary function is to prepare, to "open" himself, in order that he may receive the direction which God gives. Knowledge and appreciation of the profound importance of this principle will reinforce my serious commitment to live as Jesus did.

It is God who is the giver of all gifts; man the receiver. In other words, if I have by my "activity" responded to God's first invitation to conversion and meditated on my sins, then I will subsequently answer his next call by expressing my sorrow in some active way. The purpose of man's activity is to act on God's initial call by cultivating the soil of his heart and mind so that he may be receptive to the will of our Lord, and even under the most trying circumstances, ready and willing to await his inspiration. This waiting is essential. God gives freely, and in his own time. He will neither be rushed nor dictated to.

It is precisely this delay which we find so difficult. Here again since we are accustomed to instant results, we have little control over our impatience and soon tire of waiting — whereupon we quickly decide that our soil is sufficiently well prepared because we are ready. At this point our technological mentality asserts itself along with the temptation to believe that we can end this painful inactivity by producing for ourselves the gift we seek from God. Losing our perspective on our place in the created order, we attempt to assume the role of God.

This inclination to over-step our proper role in life is the most subtle of all temptations. As with many inducements, it begins with a truth, or perhaps more often a half-truth. Humanity is indeed called to identify with God, to become "God-like." The more we enhance through loving surrender to him that likeness of God which we possess by our creation, the more God-like we become. That is a good and desirable thing. But presuming on God's role in our lives is wrong. A son often resembles his natural father in such a way that one can say with justification that they are identical. However, no one would confuse the two or render them indistinguishable in their relationships and roles. Yielding to the temptation to do precisely that caused the fall of Adam and Eve.

On the face of it, the serpent's proposal to Eve is not only attractive; it appears as well to be harmless and even fitting. It is an extremely subtle allurement.

God had given Adam and Eve everything. They lacked no earthly possession or delight; they suffered no loss or privation: spiritual, psychological or material, for all they had, even life itself, was a gift of God.

To demonstrate their unique nature and role in his creation, their status as sharers of his own life, made in his image, God does a striking thing — he puts them in charge of all the rest of his creation (cf. Genesis 1:28-30). There is only one restriction. They are not to eat fruit from the tree of knowledge of good and evil growing in the center of the garden.

That restriction is crucial however. The continuation of their primordial relationship to God and his creation depends on their observance of it. This condition is the line of demarcation. On one side lies life and continued happiness; on the other death — the beginning of misery and sorrow and sin. The restriction exists to remind Adam and Eve that for all their gifts, for all their sharing in God's life and likeness, there remains a role and function which is proper to God alone.

It is highly unlikely that God would turn his creation over to a pair of puppets, no matter how beautifully formed. Adam and Eve were not automatons. Nor were they wide-eyed children playing in the garden. They were endowed with the perfection of human intelligence and were well aware of the beauty, goodness and intrinsic desirability of their own creation as well as of God's world around them.

When Eve listens to the serpent she sees his words as an invitation to self-completion. It is a cunning temptation. Attracted as Eve is, perhaps even enthralled by the beauty of her creation, it is normal that she should want this beauty in its fullness. "Here is the way," says the serpent. "Eat of this tree and you will truly be like gods." In her desire to be as like God as possible, Eve eats. "When the woman saw that the fruit of the tree was good to eat, and that it was pleasing to the eye and tempting to contemplate, she took some and ate it" (Genesis 3:6).

Eve, of course, is misled through the deviousness of the serpent whose denial of the true conse-

113

quences of her action constitutes an important part of the temptation.

Eve's mistake, and subsequently Adam's, is not her wish to be more like God. Wanting to be God-like is a highly desirable objective. Eve's fault is that she allowed her desire to become overwhelming with disastrous consequences. By eating the fruit which does not come to her in the form of a gift, she usurps God's role. It is as if she thought: "I know my present likeness to God, my uniqueness, my present happiness. I want these more completely. Therefore *I will make myself more* like God. I will eat of his tree."

The gift Eve seeks is really that total union with God for which we are all created. However, she goes about it in exactly the wrong way. She disobeys, tries to force God's hand. Rejection of God's will in our lives, even when it is not sinful, does not foster union. It separates. Adam and Eve do not move closer to God; they draw away from him. Having eaten God's "food," they do not become more God-like but are filled with selfishness.

Man can never force union with God. He can only love it into existence. Man's love will foster his alliance with God only when it is supported by a firm commitment to his will as revealed in our individual lives. To keep God's commands means much more than avoiding sin. Most especially, it involves a willingness to remain open to God's will; a desire to submit in trust to the love of the Father, and to be led by God, completely at peace with his decisions.

When Jesus says to his disciples, "I have food to eat of which you know nothing" (John 4:31), this is the "food" he means. "My food is to do the will of him who sent me and to finish his work" (John 4:31-38). Jesus' uniqueness lies in his total receptivity, openness, submission and perfect obedience to the Father's will which was the very essence, mainspring and core, the dynamic and moving power of his life. In spite of the problems Jesus encountered, whatever God asked of him, he accepted. His love union with the Father enabled him to trust completely. "I always do what is pleasing to him" (John 8:29).

This is Jesus' great legacy to us who would follow in his footsteps: "If any man love me, the Father and I will come to him and will reside in him" (cf. John 14:23-24). And Jesus explains what he means by "loving" him. "If you love me, you will keep my commands" (John 14:23). In other words, if we truly love him, we will live as Jesus did, in total receptivity to God's will in our lives.

The high-point, the zenith of that openness to God's will, comes for Jesus at the hour of his Passion, His Death and Resurrection. The Father willed not only this suffering, but the time of its occurrence as well. Jesus often assures his followers that the time of his Passion, that hour determined by his Father, had not come, but when it did, he received it with total obedience to the will of God. By that act Jesus repairs the disobedience of Eden. Man has come full-circle. It is the hour of triumph for Jesus and, in him, for us all. As a result of his receptivity, Jesus will once more be honored with the glory which he had in the Father before the world began.

When we receive Jesus in the Eucharist, we unite as well with the Father and the Spirit and by that union we "sacramentalize," concretize all those intangible acts of our daily lives which by our obedience to his will unite us in love with God through his divine Son.

To achieve union with God on the deepest level through Eucharistic sharing in the Body and Blood of the Lord, I must willingly allow this food to penetrate and reinforce my being as I pledge my obedience to the Father's will.

"Food" is a well-chosen symbol. If we are to strengthen our alliance of love with our God, it is essential that we let him enter our being in the same profound and mysterious way that natural food enters our life stream. As we freely receive the nourishment which sustains us, we even more openly and thankfully accept the food of God, our greatest gift and spiritual sustenance.

When we eat natural food, we assimilate it gaining the strength we need to live. When we eat of "the bread of life," we are imbued with the strength to live lives transformed by love: more open to the Father, more conscious of his presence, more in love with him.

This fullness of Eucharistic sharing demands openness, understanding and willingness on our part. God asks us to make room, to clear space so that he can transform us with his knowledge, goodness, and love. If I am filled with self, there can be no room for God. To truly have life, I must willingly surrender my blindness to God's vision, my ignorance to his wisdom, my selfishness to his love, my pride to his truth, my self-sufficiency to his power. Like the Good Servant — confidently ready and waiting to receive him — I must be grateful for his love and always willing to follow his lead.

If I would live as Jesus did, I must, in all things surrender myself to the will of the Father in prayer, continually watching and waiting for that "hour" when God will come to me, draw me closer to himself and confirm in me yet more fully his own image and likeness.

> "Wait for the Lord with patience; be stouthearted and wait for the Lord" (Psalm 27).

15

Joy

As I said in a previous chapter, the basis of Christian joy is always hope. Our joy in the Lord must be born from that reassurance which is ours because of our hope in him.

There is perhaps no more elusive a human quality or condition than joy, which can only truly be learned by experience. Joy, that deep-seated peace which is the fruit of suffering lovingly overcome, brings with it a profound sense of calm, gentleness, inner stability and reassurance. It opens one's eyes to optimism, beauty, hope and goodness. Christian joy is never superficial; it lies deep within us and is not easily destroyed. Such joy is the product of a strong love for Jesus and the Father. It enables one to see beneath the surface of events and things and find their true meaning and place in the plan of God. This joy is the Spirit dwelling in us, the fulfillment of God's promise: "If any man love me, the Father and I will come to him and make our home in him" (John 14:23). Once found, such joy can only be lost by a deliberate rejection of love on our part.

No man can take it from us.

Christian joy does not demand the absence of suffering. It is suffering overcome, not suffering avoided. Often in the intensity of the suffering, fear, and doubt which are the birth pangs of Christian joy, our temptation is to question its value. Is this happy emotion worth all that one must endure to possess it? Is this "pearl of great value" worth selling everything to obtain? Our first answer can often be "no!"

It takes great faith to persevere in our search for joy. It is easy to lose hope in the midst of all our struggles for self-mastery, as we strive to find in Jesus true peace and love. When the struggle is excessively difficult or prolonged, we are tempted to stop trusting in the Lord and to seek elsewhere for that inner peace and joy we so desperately desire. Faced with this temptation we must pray more earnestly for the grace to believe that our sorrow will indeed someday be turned into joy. The secret is not to give up but to persevere more strongly. Like everything else, true joy has its price.

Our Lord warned us of the temptation to withdraw from our pain and seek our joy elsewhere. "You will suffer and mourn but the world will rejoice" (John 16:20). The "world" seeks its joy not by overcoming pain but by avoiding it and beckons us to do likewise to escape all the intense and very real suffering of life: our loneliness, despair, sense of purposelessness and valuelessness; the devastating perception of ourselves as unloved and unloveable; our terrifying fear of loss of love, of success, of life itself — all can be escaped. In escaping them instead of bearing them we find a certain "joy."

But this "joy" is harmful. It stops growth, leaving us emotionally and spiritually immature. All the tragic escapisms at our command can bring us at best only temporary relief. They cure nothing but in fact deepen the pain. They can never bring us true peace or joy.

True suffering, that which is of God and calls me to live up to the image he has of me, which is for my good and the welfare of others — that suffering never destroys real Christian joy. What effectively destroyed Christian joy for me was not the growth-suffering to which the Lord called me so intensely at one stage of my life. What actually destroyed my peace, shattered my hope and ruined my joy were all the tragic escapisms I used to avoid pain, to avoid knowing myself and realizing how very much I am loved in spite of or perhaps because of who I am. They brought no peace because they held no truth. The agony of these escapisms was born of the lies they are. Once I learned that, growth in truth became possible. As I learned to deal with my fears and doubts with courage and trust, the joy of enlightenment returned to my life. Sometimes even now this joy dims. Every so often something will trigger anew the agony of those dark days and nights. But the agony is less vivid now, the pain less intense — more remembered than felt. It no longer destroys my peace or joy, because it has ceased to destroy my trust in the Father's love for me of which suffering is but a real and valid sign.

Pain is the seed of growth enabling us to attain fulfillment through our Father's love. Loving even in the midst of our tears; leaving behind the fantasy and delusion of youth to embrace adulthood where genuine happiness awaits us; possessing that fullness of joy to which we are summoned and entering with faith and courage through the gate of suffering — all these are the characteristic signs of the true Christian. "For was it not necessary for the Christ to suffer and so enter his glory?" (Luke 24:26). The door to our joy is Jesus.

"The joy I give you the world cannot give" (John 16:20). In following Christ our lives will in every respect be harder than if we lived for ourselves but at the same time they will be richer, more beautiful and happier. Those of us who follow him therefore are led into an unrest such as the world does not know but obtain from it a joy the world cannot give. We know that the Father loves us with an everlasting love through which all things work together for our good. So even in our suffering, there is always hope, an unshakable hope, born of our conviction, faith and trust in his love. Our joy can be diminished only when we let ourselves be numbered with those of little faith. We have no real cause ever to do that!

Joy in the Lord can never be faked nor can it be self-induced. It always exists in us as gift, seen in our eyes, heard in our laughter, found in our attitude to stress and adversity. It causes us to do strange things at which the "world" can only wonder, uncomprehendingly. In our joy we stand in awe and unfeigned delight before the marvels of God's creation. With deepened vision, allowing us to see goodness and beauty where others see only squalidness and misery, we experience hope in the midst of despair. Through the power of this joy we may perceive God's loving and eternal plan in the events and movements of history. The truth and glory of this world renewed, transformed and redeemed by love are reflected in the light of our joy. We come to know as well our own worth and beauty and because of all we see, rejoice.

This is the joy Jesus knew. He shows it all his life. It is impossible to read the accounts of Jesus' agony in the Garden of Gethsemane without being moved by the sense of peace, and joy, which follow that suffering. To miss that is really to miss the entire message.

Our joy in the Lord will always be a reflection of the intensity of our faith and commitment to love. The more deeply and fully we are dedicated, to loving as Jesus did, the greater will be our joy. Our message to our world is that this complete and perfect joy is possible.

We have an obligation to bring joy into the world. This is an integral part of living and loving our neighbor. Glum faces and despairing attitudes do not reflect God's love and caring concern but rather, block his good news of hope. Our neighbor has a right to the message that our hope and joy can bring him; to the knowledge that even in this time of moral decadence, darkness, pessimism, of overwhelming social problems, and personal rejection — even now, joy lives for all of us in the Father's love.

Spreading the spirit of joy is not as difficult as one might think. I remember one retreat where smiling at someone who was having a hard time was held up as an example of worthwhile Christian activity. Somewhat skeptical, I decided to test the validity of this theory by actually putting it into practice. Shortly afterwards an occasion presented itself. I was making a trip which called for me to change planes at the Detroit airport. It happened to be Christmastime and the usual rush and confusion prevailed. The young lady checking passengers for another flight as well as our own was being subjected to a constant barrage of complaints, repetitive questions and unkind comments. Suppressed anger and hurt were evident on her face and grew with each incident. I decided that the situation couldn't be better for a real test of the "smile" theory. Having already dealt with my own frustration, I was calm both inwardly and outwardly. One could easily see in that young lady our Lord being harried by so many wants, criticisms, demands and by such great misunderstanding.

As I checked in, I smiled and said, "I don't know how you manage to cope with all this, but

I'm sure our Lord understands."

The effect was almost miraculous. All tension visibly drained from her face, which became completely relaxed and *she smiled*.

Even though in my doubt I added a few words to the smile she received from me, I am now a convert to the power of Christian joy.

Perhaps the greatest legacy of this generation will be our gift of joy. It is sorely needed. In a world that lacked love, people once remarked: "Look how the followers of Christ love one another." How glorious it would be if in these often sad and troubled times our contemporaries could marvel: "Look how those Christians rejoice" — and in our joy find their hope.

16

Our Solitary Boast

Do we Christians fully appreciate the meaning and significance of that event known as the Annunciation? Its historical significance is that our world might well be vastly different without Mary's free assent in faith to God's invitation to be the mother of Jesus. Just what kind of life this might be and what would have happened is an academic question, open to all sorts of specula-tion. The reality is that in the fullness of her faith and freedom, Mary said: "Yes! I am the Lord's servant; as you have spoken, so be it" (Luke 1:38).

Volumes have been written on the power and beauty of that answer. It has inspired countless hours of fruitful meditation. United with Jesus' "yes," Mary's consent to the Father's will becomes another "incarnate word": the union of the human word with the divine for the salvation of men.

The beneficial effects of Mary's assent are enormous. Joined with her Son's "yes," Mary's consent to the Father's will dramatically changed the course of human history, irrevocably altered the direction of mankind's journey. To fully appreciate its importance, we must reflect upon Eden and that other event which also affected the destiny of man.

As we have seen earlier (cf. chapter 12), Eve made a selfish and drastic mistake in her quest for perfection: she let her desire rule her; she acted in disobedience. Eve's "no" to God has serious consequences. That act of refusal by a man (Adam) and a woman (Eve) determined the fortune of humanity. By our first parents, we were sent out of the garden to search laboriously for ourselves and for God. Instead of living happily in the peace and light of Eden, we were condemned to live in darkness and turmoil. Without our intimate and familiar union with God we felt alienated, separated. Answers to the riddles and perplexities of human existence, once not required, became the necessary objects of a long and arduous search. God, once so plainly seen, now remains hidden, obscured from our vision. Lost is our intended freedom: from death, suffering, disillusionment and despair.

The long-lasting effect of rejecting God in Eden was that mankind was destined to acquire a new knowledge. We were to discover for ourselves the consequences of displacing our Lord, of unwillingness to walk with him, and desire to be not servant, but master. After Eden, mankind begins its journey away from truth. The serpent's lie becomes incarnate in us. Man walks no more with his God.

But although he rejected God, man was not abandoned. Throughout the course of salvation history, God intervenes by calling his people back to him, inspiring man to reverse his steps and return. When the time for mankind's salvation approaches, God calls us back to union with himself through Abraham, Moses, and the prophets. Finally, in the fullness of time, God calls to humanity through Mary.

There is no divinity in Mary. She is completely human. So in her "yes!" one person inspires the faith that another rejected through her "no!" Because of Mary all creation is brought closer to God. Light illumines our darkness. Hope lives again, born of a new faith. The glory of the Lord once more fills our land. That is the significance of Mary's "yes" and why the Annunciation is so important.

All of salvation history is merely the formal statement of our individual personal histories. Both Eve's rejection and Mary's love of God are reflected in our behavior. In Mary our lives find true meaning and purpose. Her consent destroys the darkness of Eve's refusal; her love warms a world gone cold. Through Mary we realize the value of suffering, the place of success, sin and forgiveness in our day-to-day living and especially what it means to live as Jesus did.

"The glory of God," says Irenaeus, "is man fully alive." Surely mankind was never more completely alive or filled with divine life, than in

Mary. Her immaculate conception and the other privileges of her state do not make Mary "superhuman." In her are returned to mankind the gifts lost by Eve. She is the embodiment of the perfection we are all capable of and with God's help may someday attain.

Mary was not "locked into" obeying God. She had the same free will possessed by Eve as well as ourselves. If we more often follow Eve than Mary, it is not because we lack any unique quality inherent in Mary's "yes!" Failure in our life with Jesus stems only from our decision to become more the children of Eve than of Mary. We may freely echo her answer to God's calling in our lives and make her consent our own.

Mary, our Mother and Model, inspires us to realize that in spite of our own innate spiritual poverty, the Lord has done great things for us, as we echo her hymn of praise and gratitude to him — the Magnificat. To the consent of both Jesus and Mary, we add our "yes" so that through him, all may be presented anew to the Father.

Mary's assent to God's will is affirmed each time we respond to his calling, each time we strive to live as Jesus did — loving and obeying the Father in the knowledge that he will continue to "do great things for me."

In Adam and Eve, mankind refused God. Through Mary, humanity embraced his will. In all our history, that is our solitary boast.